I0464591

AutoIT
scripting
for
Beginners

RAJAN

AutoIT scripting for Beginners

By Rajan

© Copyright 2015

All rights reserved. No portion of this book may be reproduced or distributed in any form or by any means, or stored in a database or retrieval system, without the prior written permission of the publisher.

Preface

AutoIT is a scripting language well suited to beginners. This book is written to help you learn AutoIT in a simple and easy way. If you are an absolute beginner in programming, you'll find that this book explain complex concepts and terminology in an easy to understand manner with practical illustrations.

Since AutoIT is one of the best open source tool available in the market, now most of the IT company start using it in QA , networking and maintenance field for automating routine task. So, it will be right time to start learning AutoIT.

Writing this book has been a challenge and a pleasure. I hope that you find the same challenge and pleasure in learning AutoIT.

Contents at a Glance

What's Inside

Division Assignment Operator (/*)

Concatenation Operators

Simple Concatenation Operator (&)

Concatenation Assignment Operator (&=)

Comparison Operators

Equivalence Operator

Not Equal to Operator

Greater than operator

Greater than or equal to Operator

Lesser than operator

Lesser than or equal to Operator

Logical Operators

AND Operator

OR Operator

NOT Operator

Order of precedence

7) Selection statements

If..Then statement

If... Else Statement

If...ElseIf...Else...EndIf

Nested If statement

Select case statements

Switch Statement

8) Iteration statements

StringIsLower

String Upper

StringIsUpper

StringLen

StringIsDigit

StringLeft

StringRight

StringMid

StringInStr

StringReverse

String Replace

12) Windows functions

WinActivate

WinActive

WinClose

WinExists

WinGetClassList

WinGetHandle

WinGetState

WinGetTitle

WinKill

WinMinimizeAll

WinMinimizeAllUndo

WinSetState

WinWait

WinWaitActive

Control Click

13) Calculator Automation

Task To Perform

Pre-Requisite

Properties

Automation script

1) Introduction to AutoIT

AutoIT is an open source automation tool for Windows GUI. It has its own BASIC scripting language for writing scripts, and is typically used in the administration, Quality Assurance, Maintenance, monitoring and system management fields for automating routine tasks. AutoIT can manipulate the simulation of keyboard input, mouse movement and other controls to reliably automate tasks, unlike other programming languages.

Scripts written in AutoIT can be converted into compressed standalone executable files with the help of the Aut2Exe application, so it almost mimics Java's"Write Once and Run Anywhere"behavior. Once scripts are written and converted into executable files, they can be run on any windows systems that don't have AutoIT interpreter. This tool comes with a pre-installed SciTe editor for writing the script which has many features including syntax highlighting, syntax folding, auto complete, auto indentation etc.

Why AutoIT?

- It is available for free in the market.
- Automate all window applications.
- Non programmers can easily learn AutoIT script.
- Online forums for beginners.
- Many inbuilt functions for automation.
- It allow user to build own user defined functions.
- Compatible with all Window OS
- Simulate mouse, keyboard movements.
- Sending user inputs to individual controls in an application.
- Easy to interact with Component Object Modeling (COM) objects.
- Create Stand alone application
- Object oriented approach

- Easy debugging
- QA testing

How AutoIT works?

Users are able to interact with components such as textboxes, radio buttons, check boxes, buttons and many other controls in applications with the help of the keyboard, mouse and human eyes. AutoIT interacts with all of these components by simulating the keyboard and mouse events. Instead of human eyes, AutoIT has its own eye called "AutoIT window info tool," which helps the programmers identify the properties of each control as they interact with it. After identifying the properties and controls of the window, the user has to write the script in Scite Editor. AutoIT converts the script into executable file or au3.

Download and installation of AutoIT

AutoIT is compatible with Windows XP, Windows Server 2003, Windows Vista, Windows Server 2008/2008 R2, Windows 7 and Windows 8. Below are instructions on how to install AutoIT:

Step 1

Navigate to https://www.autoitscript.com/site/autoit/downloads/ and download the most recent version by clicking "Download AutoIT." You can also download AutoIT as a zip package (which doesn't need installation), but it is recommended that you download the executable file.

Software	Download

AutoIt Full Installation. Includes x86 and x64 components, and:
- **AutoIt** program files, documentation and examples.

- **Aut2Exe** – Script to executable converter. Convert your scripts into standalone .exe files!

- **AutoItX** – DLL/COM control. Add AutoIt features to your favorite programming and scripting languages! Also features a C# assembly and PowerShell CmdLets.

- **Editor** – A cut down version of the SciTE script editor package to get started. Download the package below for the full version!

Fig 1.1 AutoIT download page

Step 2

Save the downloaded file anywhere in your local drive for installation

Name	Date modified	Type	Size
autoit-v3-setup	4/3/2015 3:31 AM	Application	11,600 KB

Fig1.2 AutoIT set up file

Step 3

Start installing the file and click the"Next" button

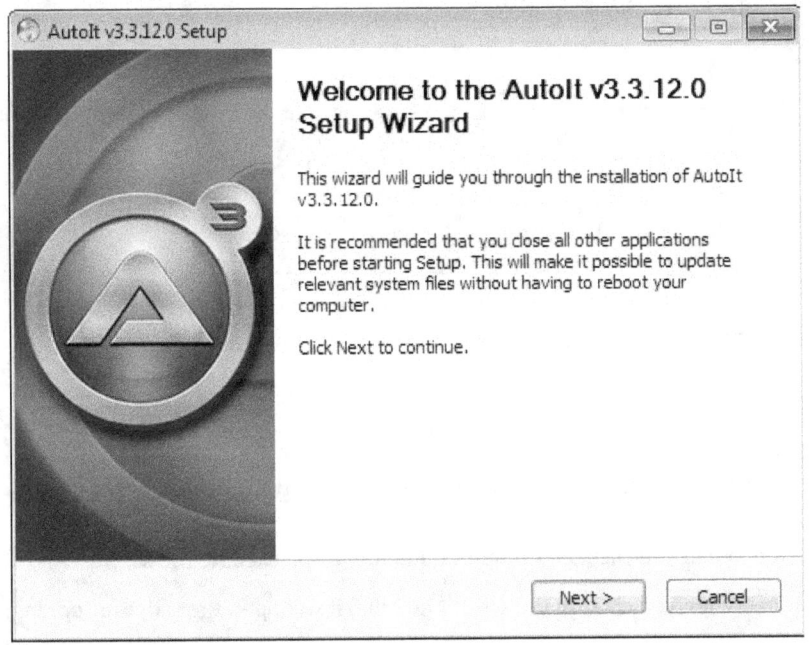

Fig 1.3 AutoIT installation window 1

Step 4

Click on the "I agree" button

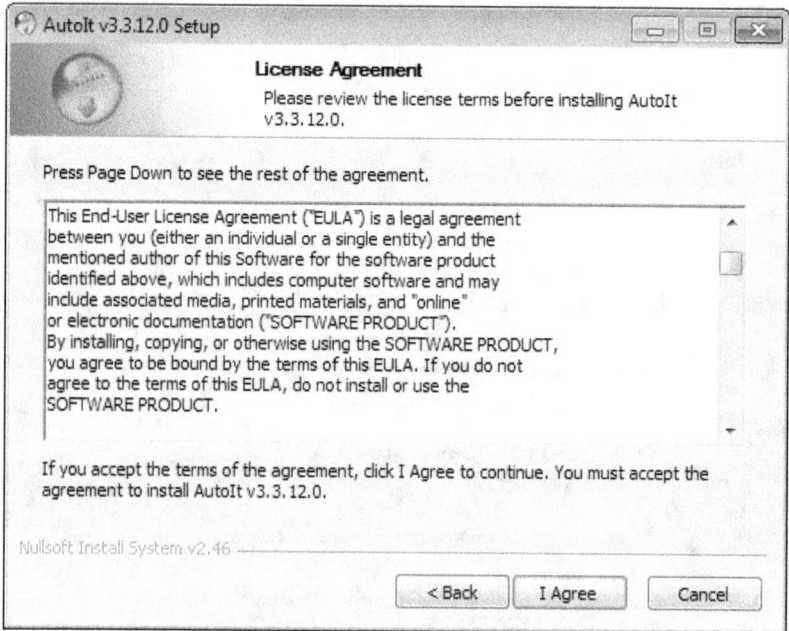

Fig 1.4 AutoIT installation window 2

Step 5

Choose the option most convenient to you and click the "Next" button.

- *Run the script*- When you click on the script (.au3 file) it will execute the script
- *Edit the script*- When you click on the script (.au3 file) it will open the script for editing.

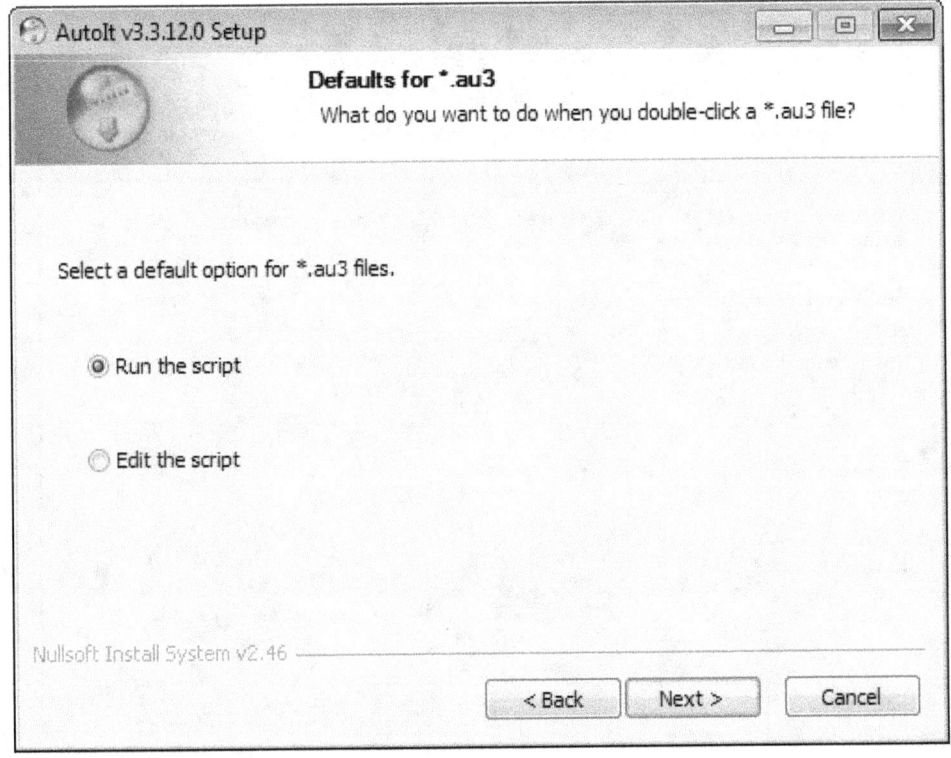

Fig 1.5 AutoIT installation window 3

Step 6

You can check both of the options for reference and click the "Next" button.

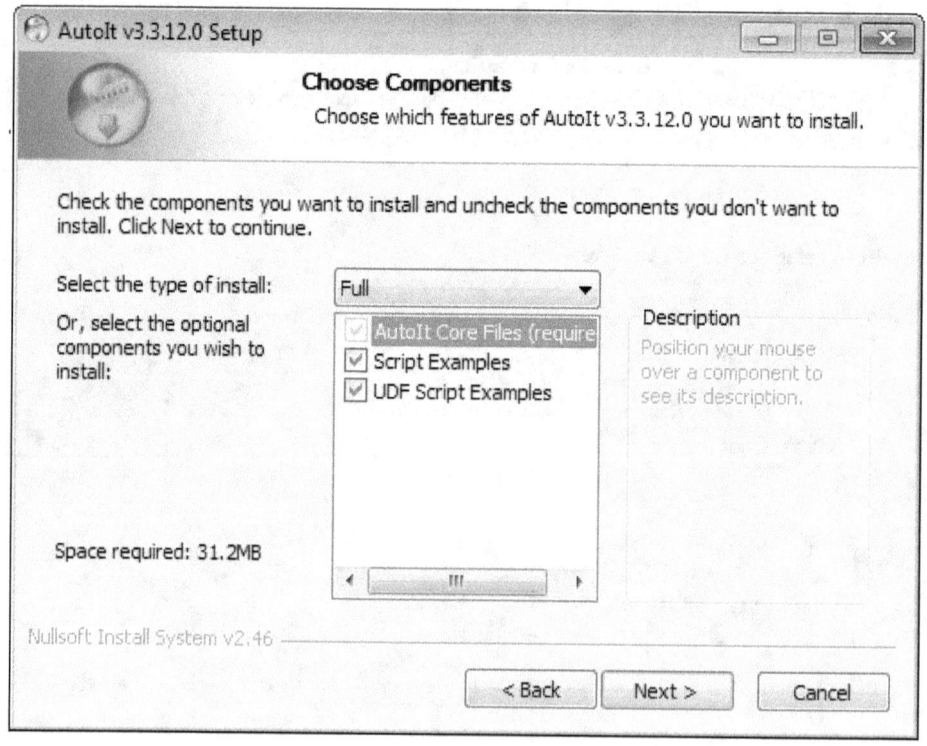

Fig 1.6 AutoIT installation window 4

Step 7

Choose the destination folder for AutoIT's installation and click the "Next" button.

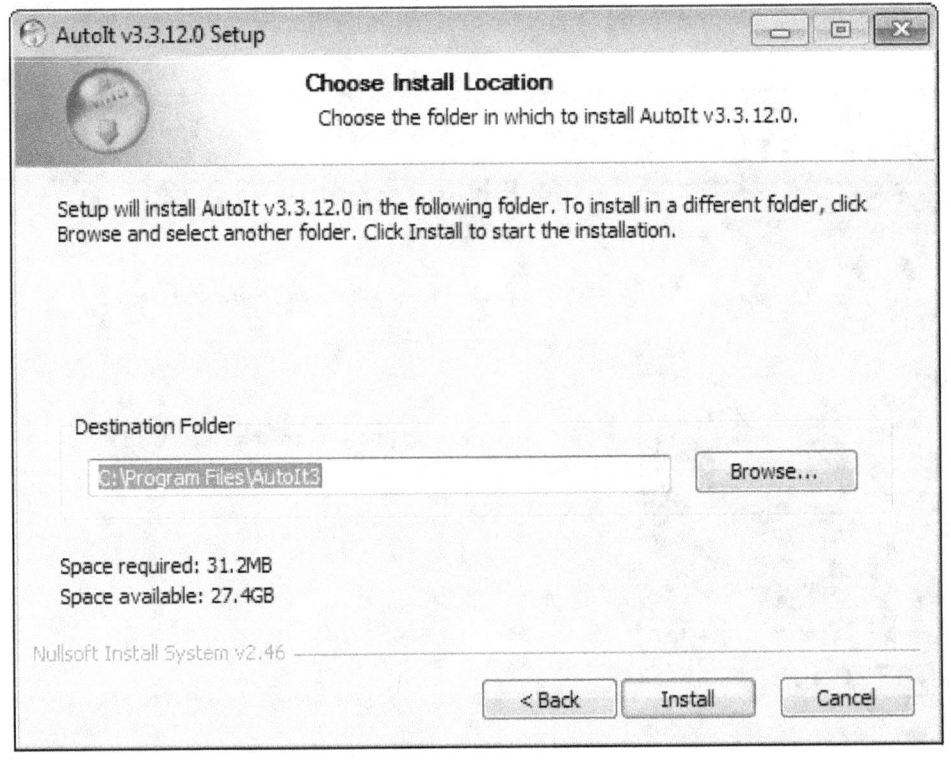

Fig 1.7 AutoIT installation window 5

Step 8

Click on the "Finish" button to complete the installation.

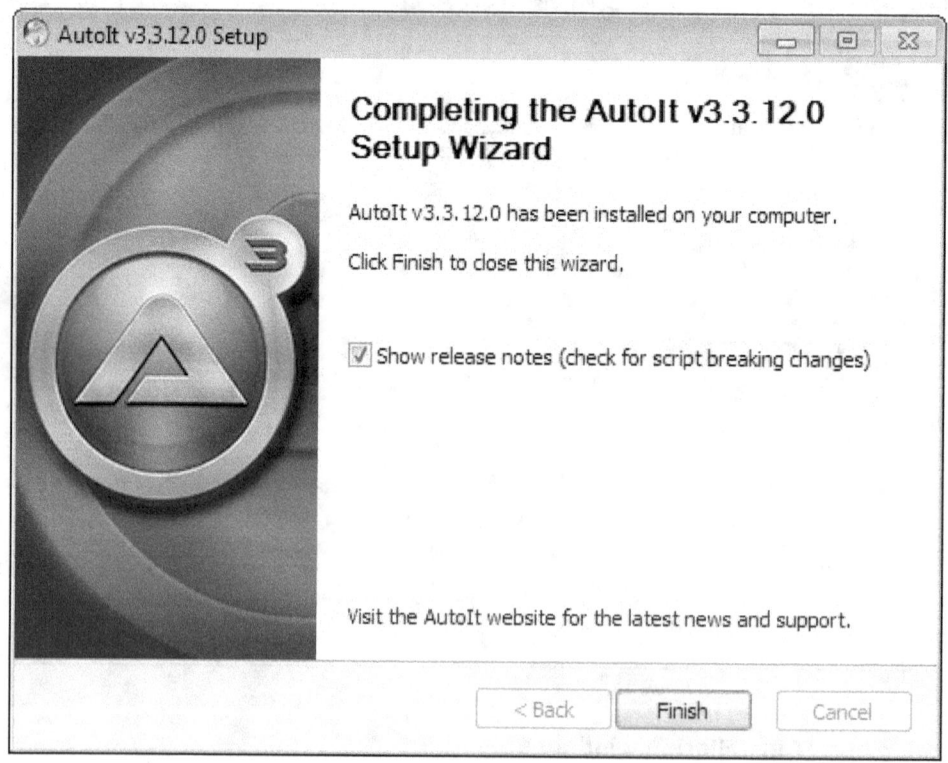

Fig 1.8 AutoIT installation window 6

Congratulations! AutoIt is now successfully installed on your machine.

2) Record and Play back

AutoIT comes with additional features called "Record" and "Play back." This Record and Play back option is helpful for identifying the objects in windows. It generates the script by identifying the mouse coordinate and windows text based on the actions of the user. When we compile the script, it again simulates those actions.

- To open Record and Play back window Go To *Start->All Programs->Autolt v3->Extras->Browse Extras->Au3Record.*

You can find an application named "Au3Record." Launch it.

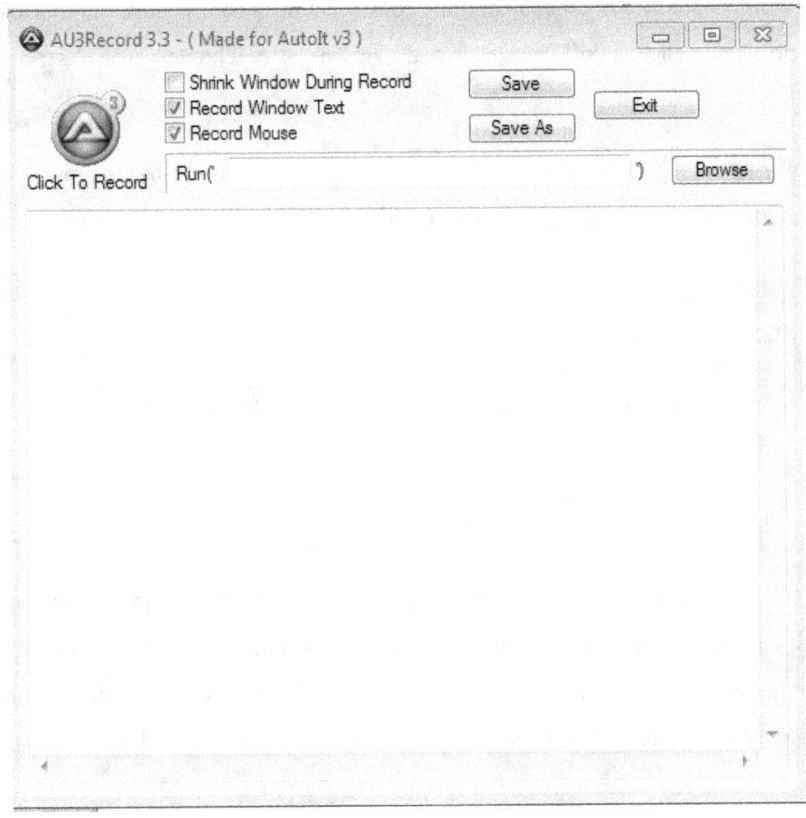

Fig 2.1 Au3 Record window

Click to record-After the user clicks on the "Click to Record" button, the Recorder starts recording actions.

Shrink window During Record-When this check box is enabled, it minimizes this record window during recording.

Record Window Text-When this check box is enabled, the recorder generates the script by referencing the currently recording application's title and text.

Record Mouse-When this check box is enabled, it includes the mouse coordinates, number of clicks and type of click (left, right and middle click) in the script.

This record and play back feature has the option to launch the application to be recorded by referencing the source file or simply by activating the application already launched and minimized in the taskbar.

How to record and play back?

Let's launch the simple calculator application and play with it. To do this, follow the steps below:

Step 1

You need to find the location where your calc.exe file is stored in C:\ Drive. I found mine in the path *C:\Windows\System32,* but it may vary depending upon different windows and OS versions. An easy way to find the location is to enter "Calc" in the Start task bar. The calculator application will be displayed. Right-click on it and select "Open file location" to find the path.

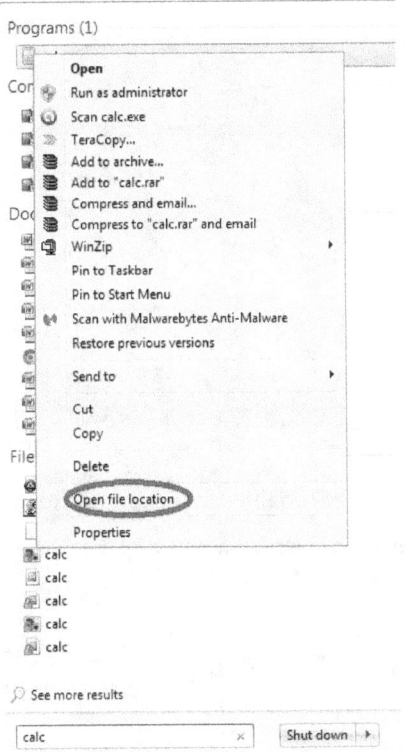

Fig 2.2 Finding calculator location

Step 2

Launch "RecordAu3" recorder available in the path *Start->All Programs->AutoIt v3->Extras-> Browse Extras->Au3Record.*

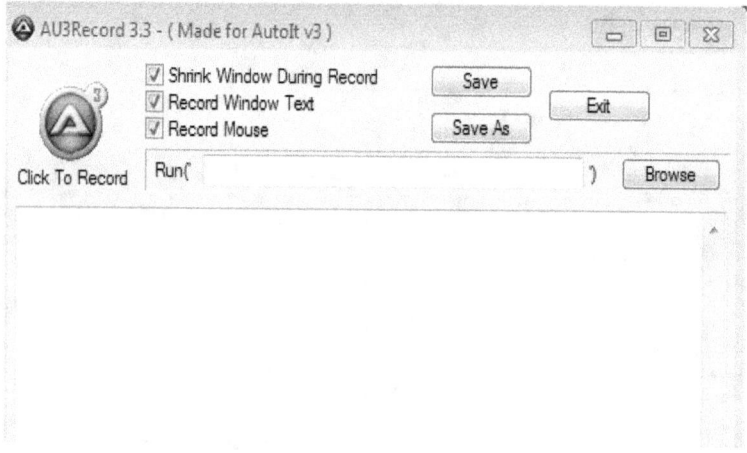

Fig 2.3 Launching Au3 Record window

Step 3

Click the "Browse" button and an open file dialog box will appear on the screen. Navigate to the path where your Calc.exe is located and select the calc.exe file. The path will be displayed in the Run text box as shown below:

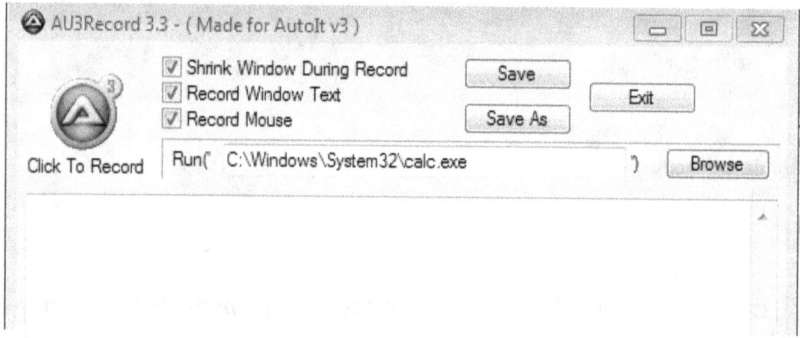

Fig 2.4 Launching calculator using Browse button

- Note: If you already launched the Calculator window, then you can skip this step and activate the minimized Calculator window.

Step 4

It's recommended to enable all three Check boxes:"Shrink Window during Record,""Record Window Text" and "Record Mouse." Then, click on the "Click to Record" button. The Calculator window will be launched as soon as you click that button, as shown below:

Fig 2.5 Recording calculator

If your application controls like text box or button lie behind the "Click to stop" button, then you can move the button to either the right or the left by placing the cursor on the arrow mark(Encircled in the Fig).

Step 5

After the Calculator window appears on the screen, I'm going to perform the following actions:

1) Press button 3

2) Press button +

3) Press button 7

4) Press button =

5) Stop the recording by pressing the button "Click to stop."

Let's see the script generated for the above actions in the figure below:

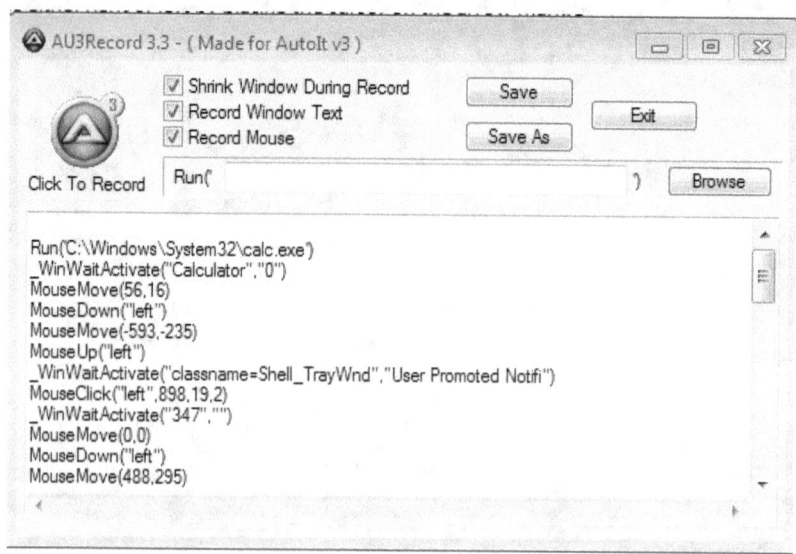

Fig 2.6 Script generated by Au3 Recorder

When you perform the same action, the mouse coordinate values will differ from user to user. As of now, there is no need to analyze the generated script. We will see each function in detail in later chapters.

Step 6

Save the script anywhere in your computer with the extension as .au3 by clicking on the "Save" button. Once you have successfully saved the script, the following message will be displayed:

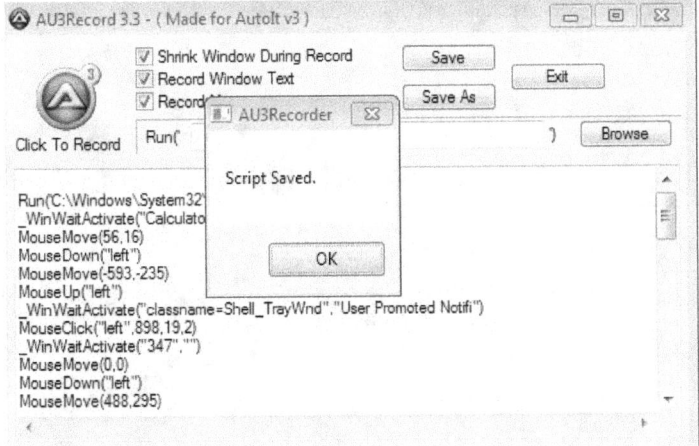

Fig 2.7 Save the script as au3 file

Step 7

Go to the path where your script is located. Double click your script to execute. It will simply perform the addition action and display the result.

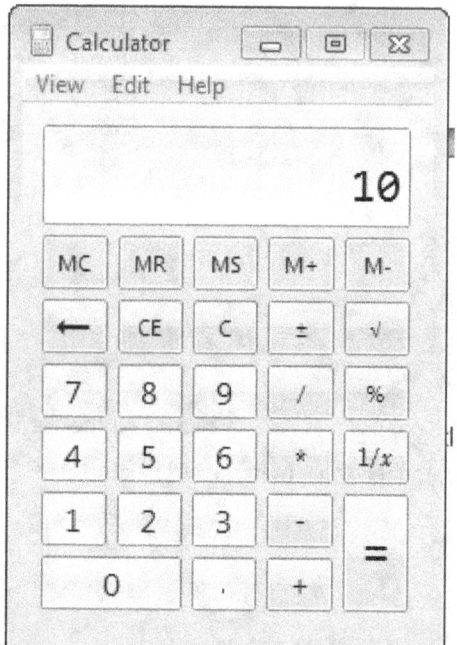

Fig 2.8 Play back the recorded script

3) AutoIT V3 Window Info Tool

AutoIT contains a standalone tool called "AutoIT V3 window Info Tool." It acts as a bridge between you and your windows applications. You don't have the power to see the properties of each window opened in your computer, but with the help of the window info tool you can easily identify the properties and objects of all windows in your computer.

What is the use of identifying properties and objects of windows?

The answer is to automate applications. To do that you need to identify the information and controls of the applications. Each and every application has its own title, class, controls, text, status bar etc., and we cannot get this information without the help of the AutoIT window info tool.

To open the window info tool, go to *Start-> All Programs->AutoIt v3->Auto It Window info tool.*

The AutoIT window info tool will be launched as shown below:

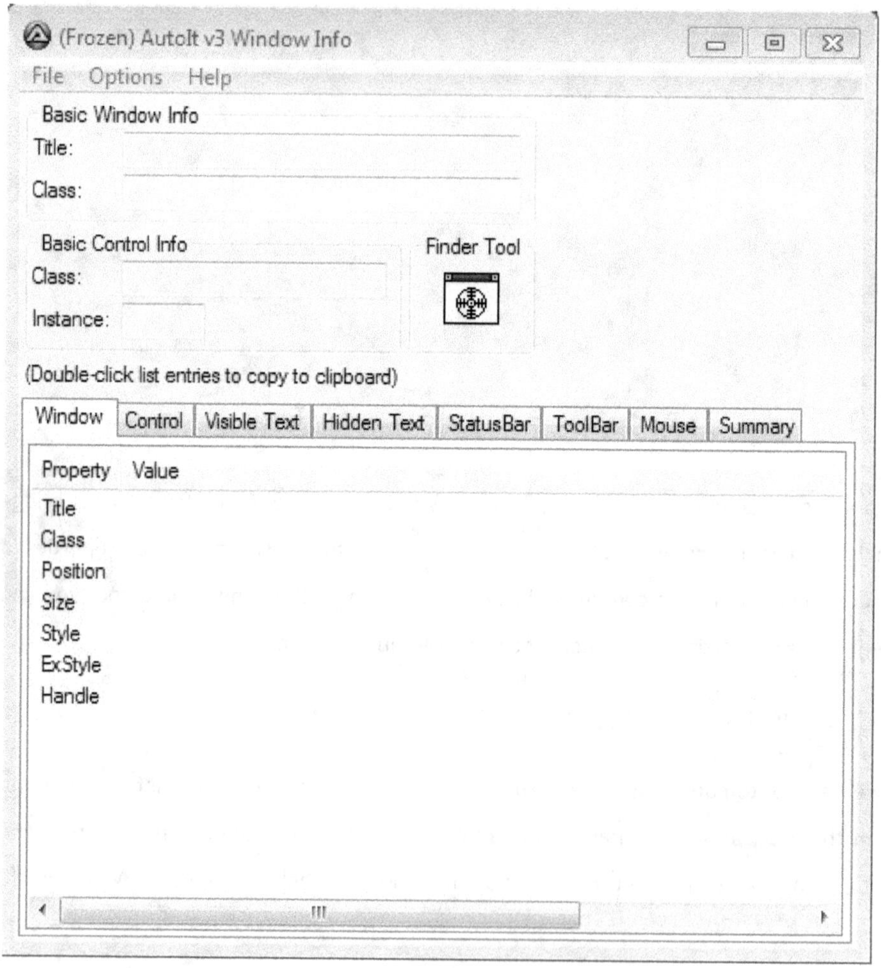

Fig 3.1 Window info tool

Let's look at the commonly used options available in the Window info tool in detail.

1) Finder Tool

Finder Tool

Fig 3.2 Finder tool

Objects can only be identified with the help of this finder tool. To do this, drag the finder tool (your mouse pointer will be turned in to the icon of the finder tool) and place it on the object you need identified. Then the object information will be displayed in this tool.

2) Basic Window Info

Basic Window Info
Title: Untitled - Notepad
Class: Notepad

Fig 3.3 Basic window frame

This displays the title and class name of the window identified by the finder tool. Each and every window has its own title name and class, but there is a chance that more than one window will have the same title and class. In that case, you need to explore other information such as the control ID, text, name, instance etc. to differentiate it. You should be aware that this basic window info frame displays the title and class of the window, not the controls.

3) Basic control Info

Basic Control Info   F
Class:
Instance:

Fig 3.4 Basic control frame

This displays the class and instance of controls identified by the finder tool. Controls are nothing but the components or objects present in the window such as Edit box, textbox, drop down box etc. Let's look at the properties of each tab in detail.

4) Window properties

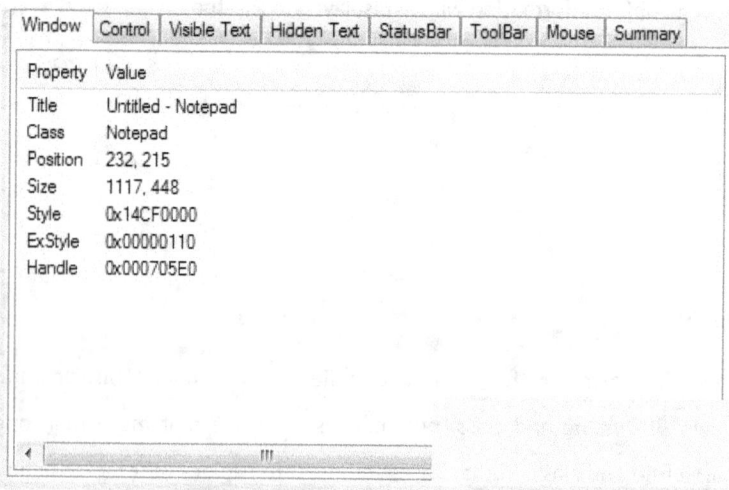

Fig 3.5 Window tab

I launched a new notepad and kept the finder tool on it, andthe Window tab in the finder tool displayed the window properties of "Untitled Notepad."

- The title denotes the window title of notepad, in this case being "Untitled- Notepad." If you save the file with any other file name, then the same name will be displayed as the title.

- Class property displays the class where it belongs to. The entire notepad file belongs to Notepad class.

- Size property displays the length and breadth of currently opened Notepad window.

- Exstyle and Handle properties indicate the style and Handle in hexadecimal value.

5) Control properties

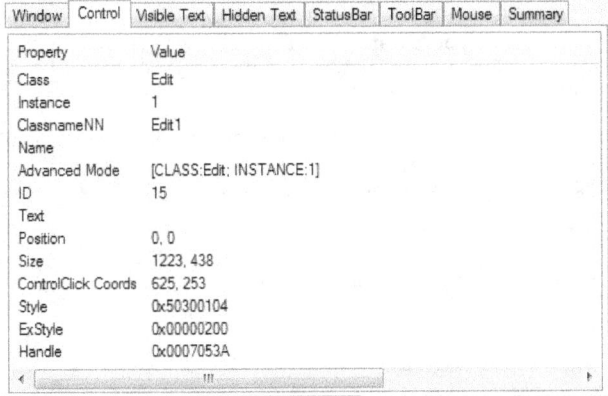

Property	Value
Class	Edit
Instance	1
ClassnameNN	Edit1
Name	
Advanced Mode	[CLASS:Edit; INSTANCE:1]
ID	15
Text	
Position	0, 0
Size	1223, 438
ControlClick Coords	625, 253
Style	0x50300104
ExStyle	0x00000200
Handle	0x0007053A

Tabs: Window | Control | Visible Text | Hidden Text | StatusBar | ToolBar | Mouse | Summary

Fig 3.6 Control tab

- Control property tab displays the properties of specified control after you drag and place the finder tool on the control.

- Class - displays the value of notepad control. Here it shows the value as "Edit" since notepad control belongs to the "Edit" class.

- Instance - AutoIt assigns an instance value starting from 1 when all of the given properties match with other controls in the same window.

- ClassnameNN- previously used in the old version of AutoIT. This no longer exists.

- Name- displays the Winform name assigned to control when it's developed in the .Net framework.

- Advanced Mode: usually displays the class and instance of controls.

- ID: window assigns an internal numeric ID to each control in application. (For example, it assigns Control ID 15 to Notepad. Most commonly, controls are identified by control ID.)

- Text- displays the text on the control. If you are going to get the properties of Button control, then it will have some text like "Yes" or "No," but in most cases it won't display the same text that appears on the screen, and may vary based on several parameters.

- Position- displays the x-coordinate and y-coordinate of the control with respect to the window it belongs to—not to the screen.
- Size- indicates the length and breadth of the particular control—not the whole window.
- Control Click Coordinate - displays the x-coordinate and y-coordinate of mouse with respect to the window it belongs to.
- Style, ExStyle and Handle display its value in hexadecimal format.

6) Visible Properties

This displays the text visible to the user. For example, I'm going to enter some text in the notepad window and identify it with the finder tool.

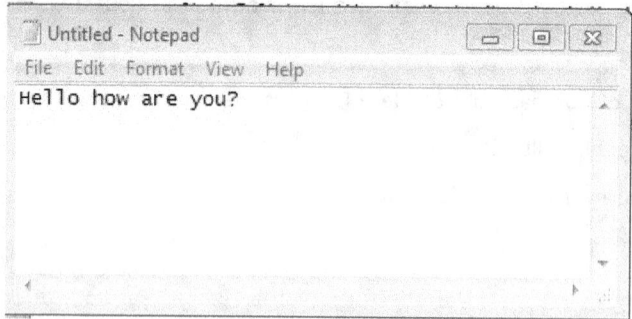

Fig 3.7 Notepad window

Text in the notepad identified by the finder tool is displayed in the visible text tab as shown below:

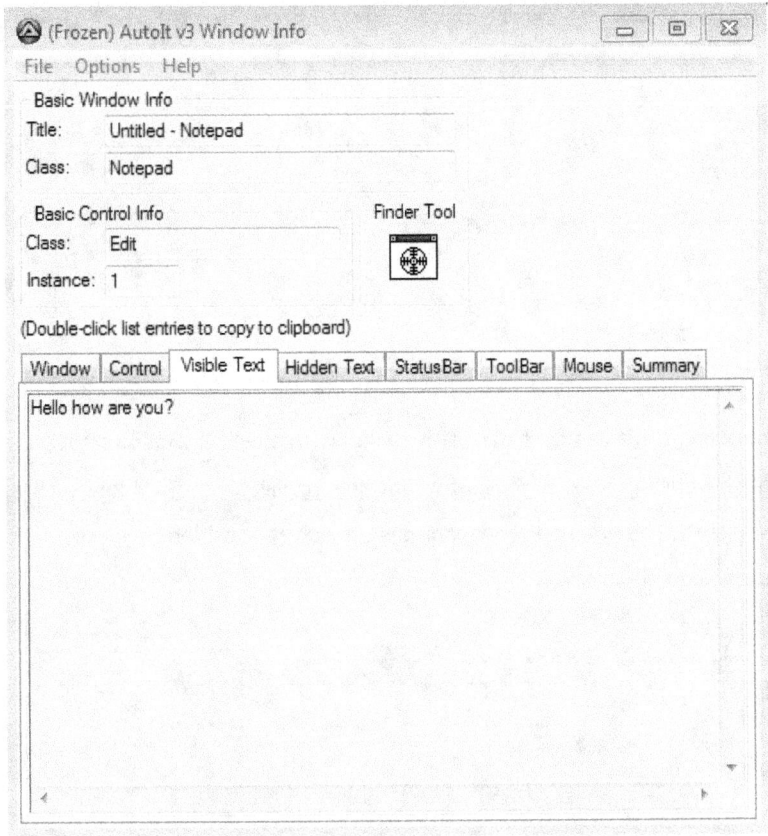

Fig 3.8 Visible text tab

7) Hidden text

This tab helps us identify text that is not visible to the user. In most cases it will be empty. Since notepad doesn't have any hidden text, it displays nothing.

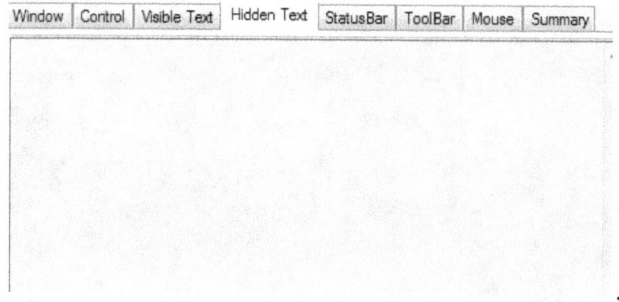

Fig 3.9 Hidden text tab

8) Status bar

This displays the text present in the status bar of the window. Almost all windows have the status bar present at the bottom side. It shows the ongoing activity of the window such as downloading, processing, etc. The notepad window displays the cursor position by specifying its line number and column number.

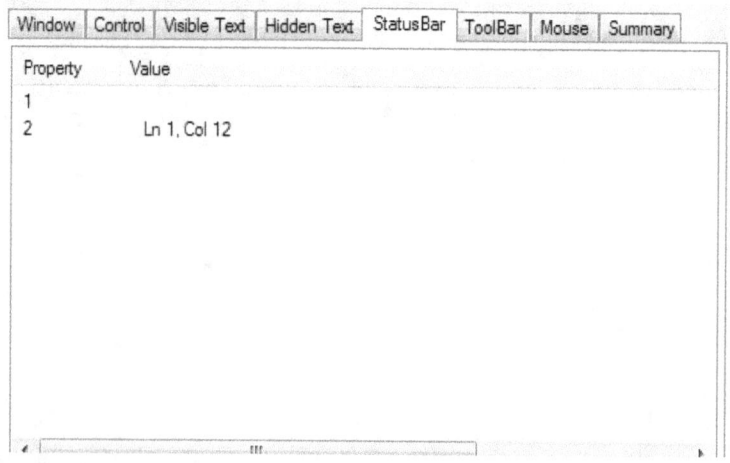

Fig 3.10 Status bar tab

9) Tool bar, mouse and Summary tab

The Tool bar tab displays the tools index, command ID and text present in it. Here, notepad doesn't have any tools to display.

The Mouse tab displays the position of the mouse co-ordinate with respect to the screen (with its origin in the top left corner), the Cursor ID (If any) and its color in hexadecimal value.

The Summary tab summarizes the values present in all of the tabs and displays it in a single tab.

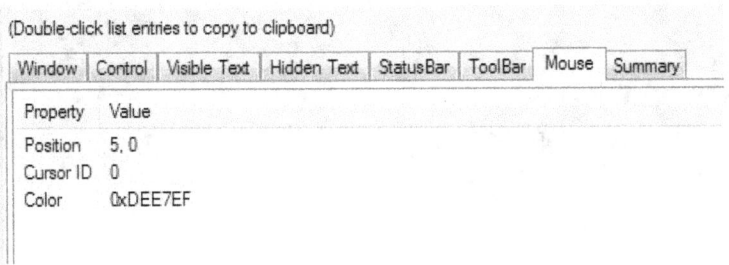

Fig 3.11 Mouse tab

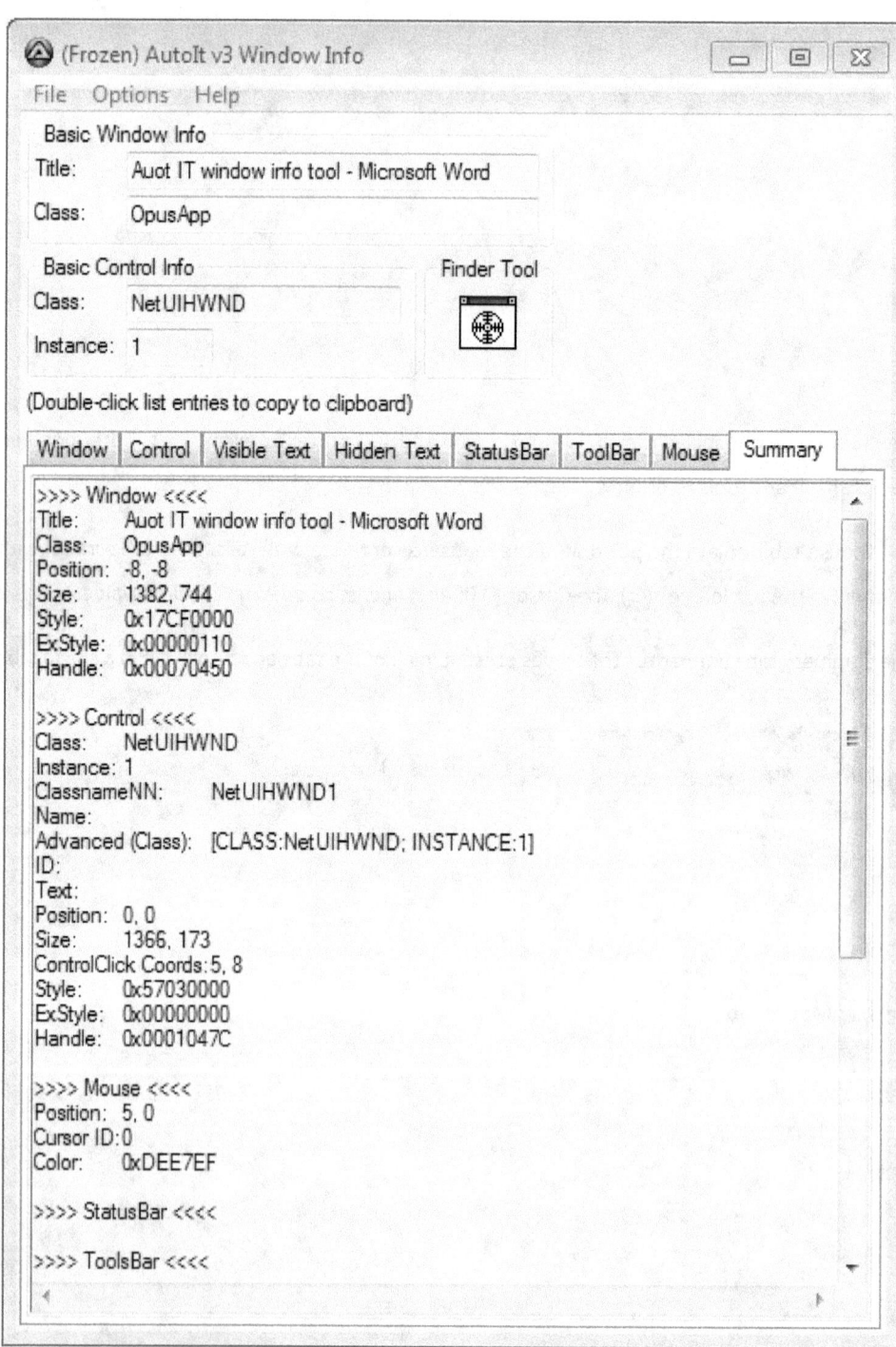

Fig 3.12 Summary tab

4) Scintilla Editor

Scintilla or SciTE Editor is an open source code editor for writing scripts. AutoIT supports this editor for script creation, and it is one of the most popularly used editors among AutoIT users. Various editors are also available in the market and supported by AutoIT but SciTE is recommend for beginners.

Other editors supported by AutoIT include:

1)Textpad

2)Crimson

3)Source Edit

4)UltraEdit

5)Notepad++

How to open new SciTE editor?

To open the new SciTE editor, Go to the Windows Explorer or folder directory where you need to save the script, right click and select *New->AutoIT v3 script* and give a file name with extension .au3. A new empty script file will be added to your destination folder. Open the file by double clicking or Right click->Open .Script. Editor will be launched as shown below:

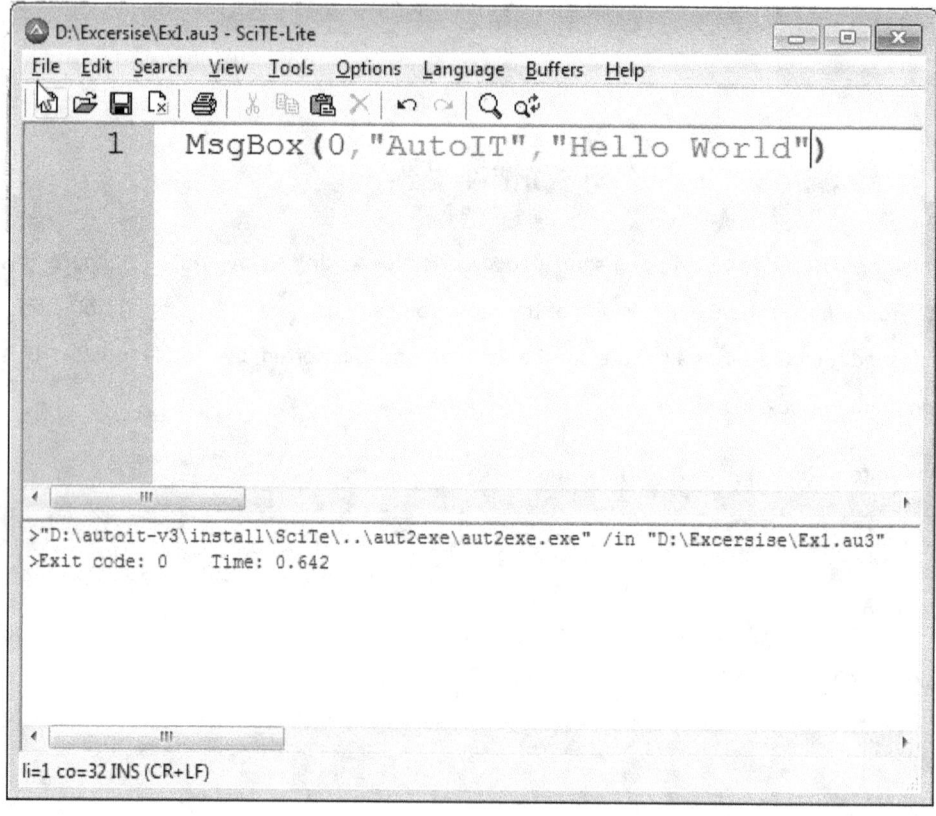

Fig 4.1 Scite Editor

Starting a new Script

Now I'm going to show a demo of how to write the script and make an.exe file out of it. I'm going to display the text "Hello world" in the message box. I will explain the functions of msgbox in later chapters, but right now you are going to learn how to use the SciTE editor. It is necessary to be comfortable with the script editor to become a pro in AutoIT.

Let's take a look at the script below:

To save the script, Go to *File-> Save* or click *Ctrl+S* and save it by entering the filename with .au3 extension anywhere in your local directory.

By using the msgbox function, we are going to display a Message box with the title "AutoIT" and content in the message box as "Hello world" with an "OK" button, but before that we have to check the syntax and create an.exe file to display the message box.

Syntax check

Before compiling the script, you need to check your syntax to find syntax errors in your script as the compiler may sometimes compile the script without giving any warning about existing syntax errors in your script.

Go to *Tools->SyntaxCheckProd* or Press *Ctrl+F5*.

After the syntax check is completed, it will display the time status and time taken at the bottom of the editor, as shown below:

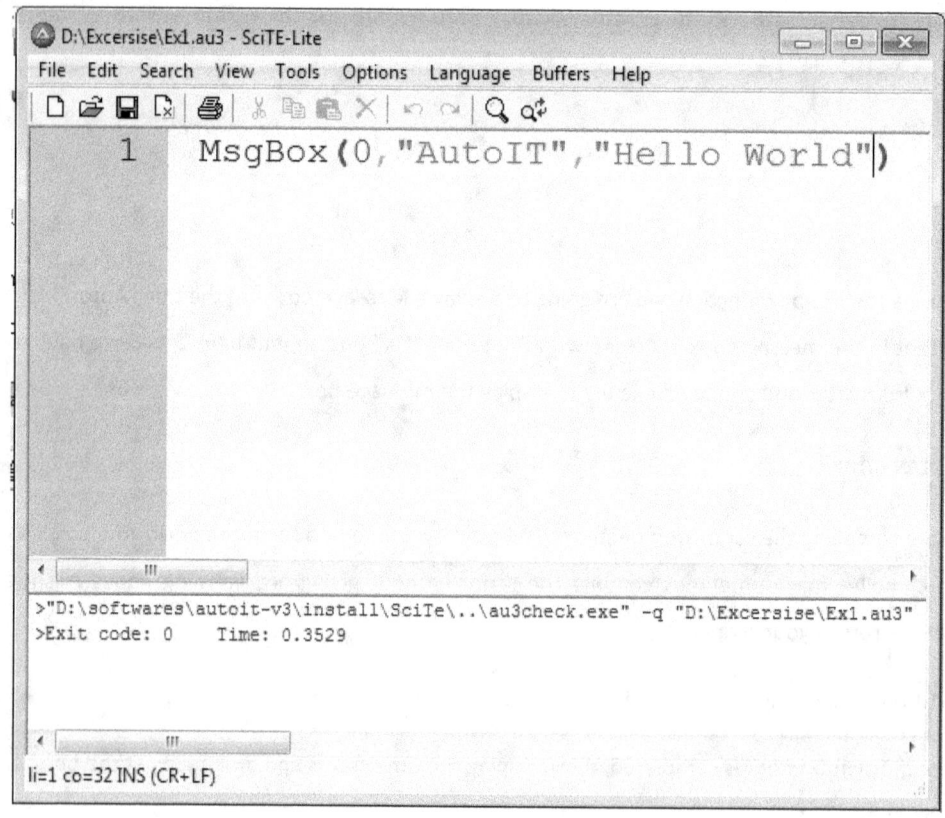

Fig 4.2 Syntax check in Scite Editor

Now we will intentionally make an error in our script to see how it identifies the syntax error. (Remember that it has the capacity to identify only the syntax error not logic ,random error, runtime error etc.)

I edit the script by adding an extra ',' after the "Hello World" and check the syntax.

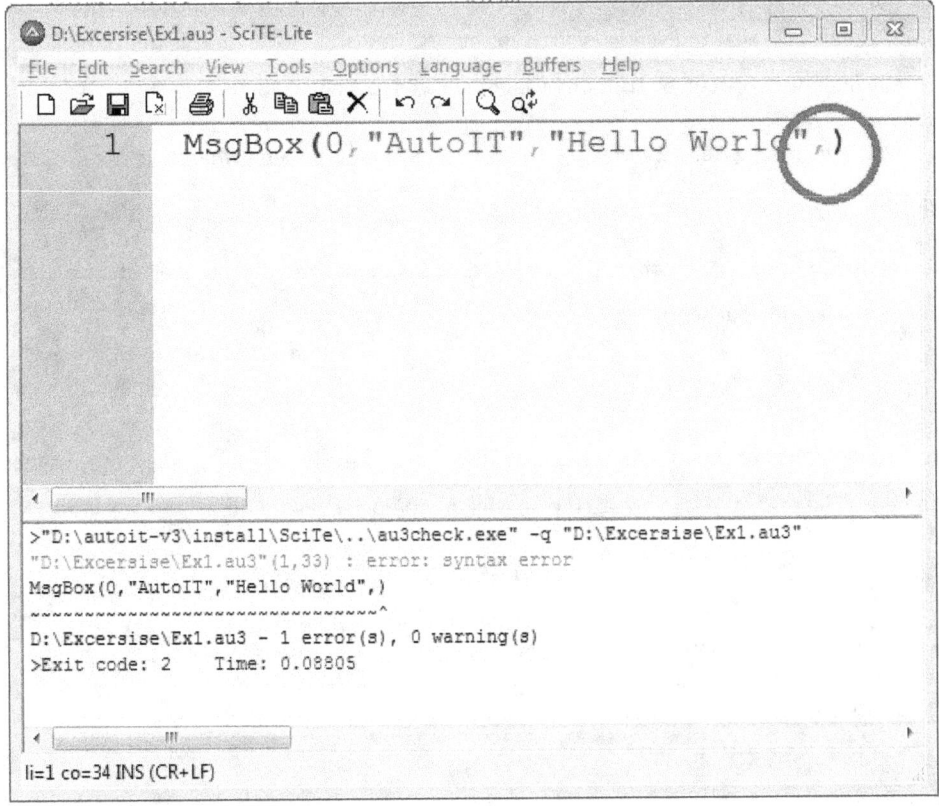

Fig 4.3 Syntax error

The error that I made in the script is encircled on the top, and you can check the syntax logic either by pressing Ctrl+F5 or SyntaxCheckProd. After the syntax check completes, it throws the syntax error message at the bottom of the editor (Encircled item). Let's look at those messages line by line.

>"D:\autoit-v3\install\SciTe\..\au3check.exe" -q "D:\Excersise\Ex1.au3""-This statement denotes that Syntax check exe is executed for the script located in the directory D:\Excercise\Ex1.au3

D:\Excersise\Ex1.au3"(1,33) : error: syntax error-This denotes the exact position where the syntax error happened in the script " by indication of its rows and column in the parenthesis

(1,35). "1" indicates that the syntax error is in the first row and "35" indicates the column. You can easily find the Syntax error position by identifying its row and column.

MsgBox(0,"Auto IT ","Hello World",)- This specifies the statement where the syntax error happened.

D:\Excercise\Ex1.au3 - 1 error(s), 0 warning(s)-This summarizes the number of errors and warnings present in your script.

Compilation

Now I have identified the syntax error and fixed it by removing the ',' from the msgbox statements. The next step is to create the .exe file by compiling my script.

To compile Go To *Tools->Compile* or click *Ctrl+F7*

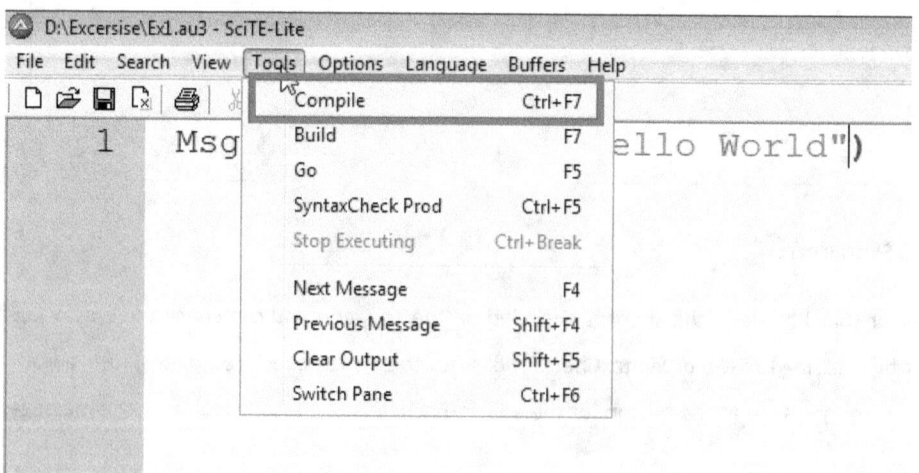

Fig 4.4 Compilation of script

Upon Compiling the script, an .exe with the same file name of my .au3 is generated in the same path. I created my .au3 file in the path D:\Excercise\so my .exe file is also generated in the same path, as shown below:

Fig 4.5 Executable file

Comments

It's necessary for programmers to add comments for the sake of their understanding as well as for reference. AutoIT comes with two types of comments, seen below:

1) Single line comments

If your comments are in single lines, then you can use semicolons in front of your comments. See the example below:

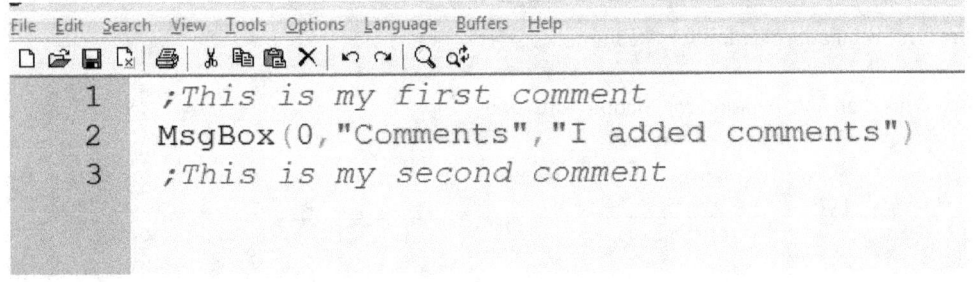

Fig 4.6 Single line comments

2) Multi line comments

In most cases, our comments exceed a line, so AutoIT comes with its own comments function to add multi line comments.

Before adding the multi-line comments, you need to include a function name called "#comments-start" at the starting line of your comment and end the comments with function "#comments-end."Be aware that even if you added a valid statement in between the "#comments-start" and "#comments-end," the compiler considers it a comment and it won't compile it.

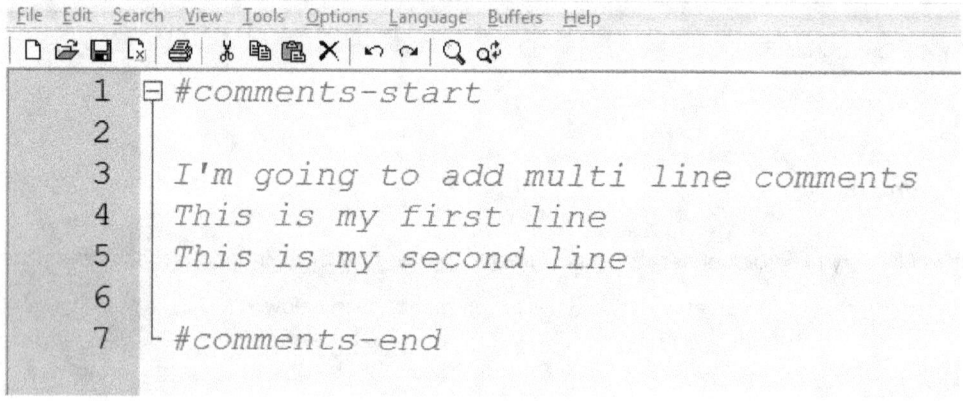

Fig 4.7 Multi line comments

You can also add comments by using the functions called "#cs" & "#ce".

#cs- This is an abbreviation for "#comments-start"

#ce- This is an abbreviation for "#comments-end"

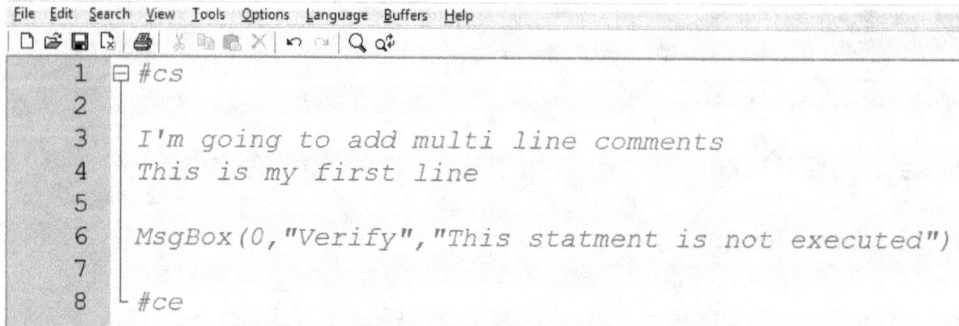

Fig 4.8 Abbreviated multi line comments

You can see that I've added a comment as well as a valid message box statement in between the #cs and #ce functions, but this message box function won't execute while the script runs because the compiler considers any statement in between #cs and #cs as a comment.

5) Declaring Variables

Variables are the stored location in the computer memory. In most cases, you cannot hard code the value in the script. For example, if you have to copy or edit some files in the directory *D:\autoit-v3\install\Aut2Exe\Icons,* then it's not recommended that you mention the same path in the script every time. You can, of course, do this,but it does not look good. You can assign the directory value to a variable and can specify that instead of giving the directory. Declaring a variable in AutoIT is very easy and comfortable when compared to other programming languages.

Naming convention of variable

AutoIT is able to identify variables only if your variable name starts with the $ symbol. So, all variables in AutoIT should starts with $ and may contain letters, numbers and/or underscores. Below are some of the examples of variable names.

$i

$value1

$string_1

Variables are case insensitive which means $value1 is the same as $VALUE1. The value assigned to the variable is stored as Variant data type. Variant data type can store any type of data like numbers, characters, objects etc.

Variable Declaration

Variables can be declared with or without three keywords called "Dim,""Global" and "Local."Let's look at each type of keyword and its scope (life time of variable) in detail.

Dim

Declaring a variable with Dim is a bit confusing and not recommended. Let's see how the keyword Dim behaves in various cases.

Case 1

If the keyword Dim is used outside any of the functions, then the scope of the variable is Global. (It can be accessed anywhere in the script)

Example 5.1

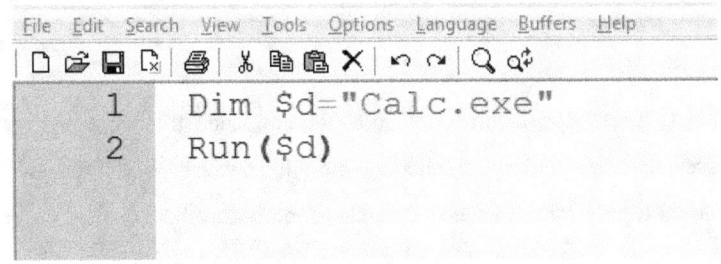

Fig 5.1 Dim used outside functions

In example 5.1, I declare a variable $prog with Dim keyword and initialize with "Calc.exe." Then I launch the new Calculator window using the Run command. (It's irrespective of where you are using the variable $prog.The value is the same everywhere in the script.) That's why we call its scope Global. When we execute the script, the calculator window will open as seen below:

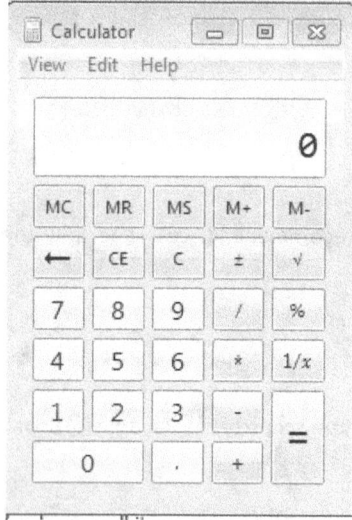

Fig 5.2 Calculator Window

Case 2

If the keyword Dim is used to declare variables within the function, then the scope of the variable is local(It can be accessible only within the function where it's declared, and if the user tries to access outside it will show an error message as Variable is not declared).

Example 5.2

File Edit Search View Tools Options Language Buffers Help

```
1    check();calling function
2
3    Func check()
4        Dim $d="Calc.exe"
5    EndFunc
6
7    Run($d)
```

Fig 5.3 Dim used inside function

Check()- This statement calls the function check(). I declared a variable called $d inside the function check() so the scope of the variable is lost once the compiler comes out of the function. In other words, the life of variable $d is lost after it compiles the last statement of the function (EndFunc). Just for demo purposes, I'm using the variable outside the function to open the calculator.When I compile the script, it will show an error message as shown below:

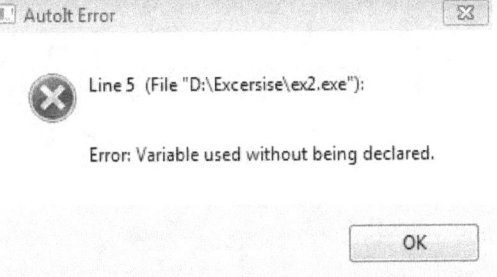

Fig 5.4 Error message

Case 3

Have you ever thought of what would happen if the same variable name (Let's say $d) is used outside and inside the function but initialized with different values? Do you think the compiler will show an error message? Absolutely Not! Let's see an example for better understanding:

Example 5.3

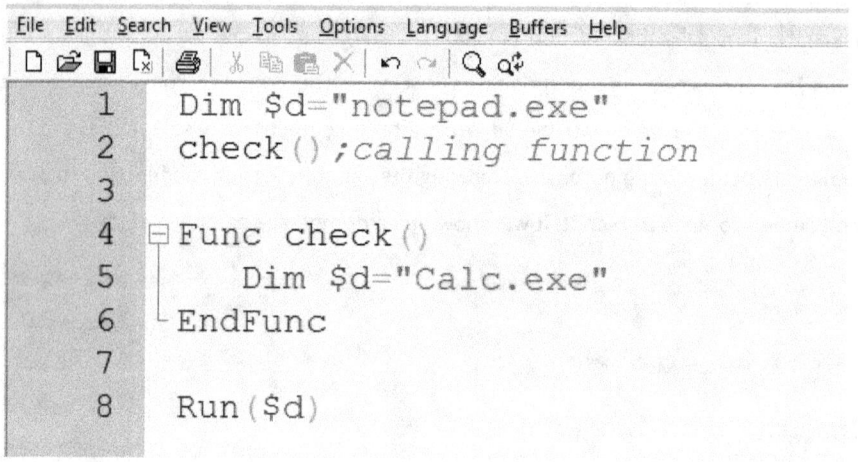

```
File  Edit  Search  View  Tools  Options  Language  Buffers  Help
1     Dim $d="notepad.exe"
2     check();calling function
3
4   ⊟ Func check()
5         Dim $d="Calc.exe"
6   └ EndFunc
7
8     Run($d)
```

Fig 5.5 Dim used inside and outside the function

In Example 5.3, I declared a variable and initialized with value "notepad.exe" outside the function and declared a variable with the same name inside the function, but initialized the variable with value "calc.exe."The Run command is used outside the function. Will notepad or calculator launch? The answer is calculator. This is why this is not recommended.

The initial value "notepad.exe" assigned to the variable was changed after the variable with value "calc.exe" within the function was executed. The Calculator window will be launched as shown below after you execute the script.

Fig 5.6 Calculator window

Case 4

We are almost done with the Dim keyword with this case. This case is simple and straightforward. The same variable is used both outside and inside the function with different values assigned to it but I didn't call the function anywhere in the script. What will happen? Let's take a look:

Example 5.4

File Edit Search View Tools Options Language Buffers Help

```
1      Dim $d="notepad.exe"
2      ;check();calling function
3
4    □ Func check()
5          Dim $d="Calc.exe"
6    └ EndFunc
7
8      Run($d)
```

Fig 5.7 Dim used inside and outside the function

I'm using the same example, but the only difference lies in the function call. I commented out the function check() with ';' so this line wont compile.Ultimately the function will not be called. When you execute the script, the notepad window will be launched as shown below:

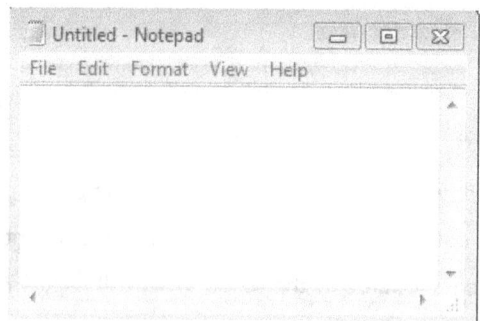

Fig 5.8 Notepad Window

Global

When you declare a variable with the Global keyword outside the function and then change its value anywhere either inside or outside the function, the variable will be altered with a new value and the variable will exist throughout the end of the script. Let's look at an example.

Example 5.5

```
  1    Global $d="notepad.exe"
  2    check(); calling function
  3
  4  ⊟ Func check()
  5  |      $d="calc.exe"
  6  └ EndFunc
  7
  8    Run($d)
```

Fig 5.9 Global statement

I'm declaring the variable $d with the keyword Global and assigning the value "notepad.exe" to it. Also, I'm altering the value assigned to the variable inside the function called check() so the value will be changed and the same will be replicated when we run using the Run command outside the function. It will launch the calculator window upon execution.

Local

The Local keyword is used to declare a variable inside the function and the life time of the variable will be destroyed once the compiler comes out of the function containing the variable. Let's look at an example.

Example 5.6

```
1      check ()
2
3    Func check ()
4          Local $a="calc.exe"
5          Run ($a)
6    EndFunc
7
```

Fig 5.10 Local Statement

In example 5.6, we declare a variable $a with the local keyword and assign a value "calc.exe" to it. You should note that we are using the Run command inside the function, so the value assigned to the variable $a will pass to the parameter of Run. Ultimately the calculator window will be launched without any issues.

Now, we will do some slight modifications to the above code by taking out the Run command inside the function and keeping it outside the function, as shown below:

Example 5.7

```
1      check ()
2
3    Func check ()
4          Local $a="calc.exe"
5    EndFunc
6
7      Run ($a)
8
9
```

Fig 5.11 Local statement

When the compiler tries to execute the above script, it will show an error message stating "variable used without being declared" because our declared variable is destroyed when the compiler comes out of the function.

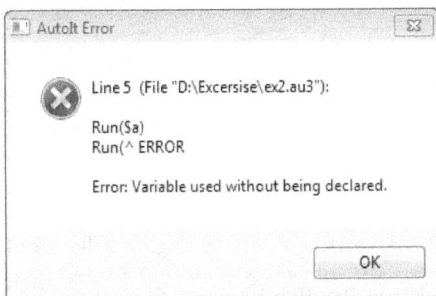

Fig 5.12 Error message

You can also declare the variable wherever you need without the use of a keyword like Dim, Local and Global, but explicit declaration is recommended.

For e.g. $value=234

Constant

Sometimes, you need to declare a variable with a constant value when you are not going to alter it anywhere in the script.For this, you can establish a keyword const. When you define the variable with the prefix as const, the value assigned to the variable will not be changed throughout the script. Let's look at an example.

Const $phi=3.14

In the above statement, we declare a variable $phi with keyword const and value 3.14. Wherever you are using the variable $phi in your script, the values will not altered. But the scope(life time) may change depending on how it's declared.(Dim, Local and Global)

Example 5.8

Let's look at a simple example for Constant:

```
File  Edit  Search  View  Tools  Options  Language  Buffers  Help

 1     Global Const $phi=3.14
 2     MsgBox(0,"value",$phi)
```

Fig 5.13 Constant statement

I declared a variable $phi globally, so the lifetime of the variable exists throughout the script. Also, I added a keyword const before the variable so it indicates that the value of the variable is constant and cannot be altered. I displayed the value with the help of Msgbox function (Understand that it is used to display the message box. We will see this in-depth in the later chapters). When you run the script, the output will be shown in the message box as seen below:

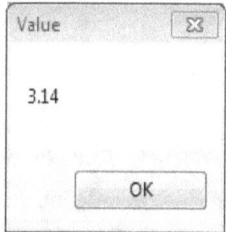

Fig 5.14 Output

What will happen if I try to alter the value of the constant variable? Do you think it will alter? The answer is no.

Example 5.9

```
File  Edit  Search  View  Tools  Options  Language  Buffers  Help

 1    Global Const $phi=3.14
 2    $phi=$phi+1
 3    MsgBox(0,"value",$phi)
```

Fig 5.15 Altering const value

I declared a constant variable and initialized with value 3.14, but in the second line I altered by incrementing the value by 1. When I compile the script, it will display an error message as shown below stating "Cannot assign values to constants."

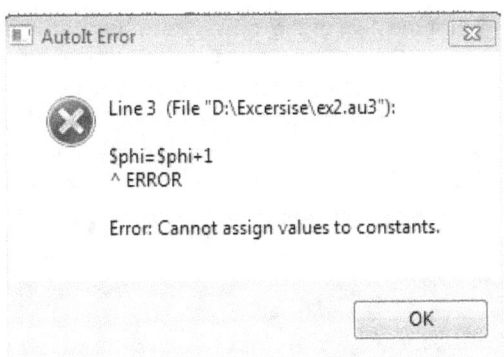

Fig 5.16 Error message

Enum

You can declare and initialize constants with the Enum keyword. It will be very helpful when you need to declare multiple constants which vary by arithmetic operations like addition, subtraction and multiplication of base variable. Below are some instances using the Enumkeyword.

If you want to create 5 constants starting with 2, with each constant incremented by 3 like 2,5,8,11,14, you can do so with the help of the Enumkeyword. See the example below:

Enum Step 3 $val1=2, $val2, $val3, $val4, $val5

I started with the Enumkeyword followed by the Step keyword, step value and then the variables. The Enumkeyword tells the compiler that this line has Enum variables. The step keyword followed by numeric (here it's 3) tells the compiler that it should increment the value by 3 by taking the starting reference from the first variable ($val1). If the variable $val1 is not initialized with a value, then the compiler assumes it as 0 and increment the second variable by 3, etc.

Example 5.10

Now, I'm going to get the value of variable $val4 with the help of the message box function and verify that it display the correct value (11).

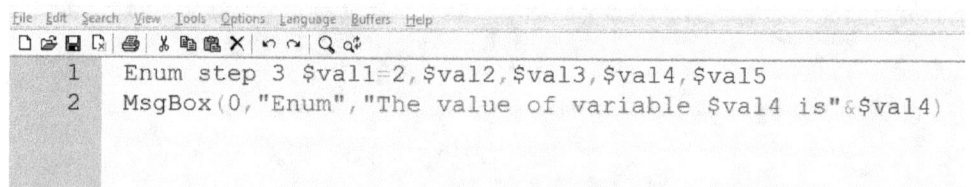

```
1    Enum step 3 $val1=2,$val2,$val3,$val4,$val5
2    MsgBox(0,"Enum","The value of variable $val4 is"&$val4)
```

Fig 5.17 Enum example

Output

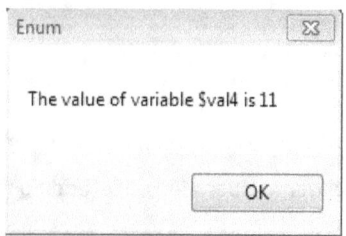

Fig 5.18 Output

If you want to create 3 constants starting with value 4 with each constant being multiplied by 3 like 4, 12, and 36, see below:

*Enum Step *3 $mul1=4, $mul2, $mul3*

Example 5.11

We are going to check whether the variable $mul3 holds the value 36 with the help of the message box function.

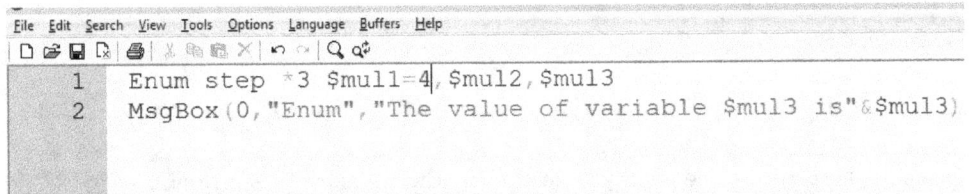

Fig 5.19 Check Enum

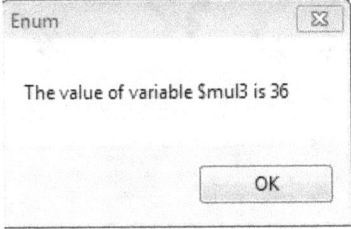

Fig 5.20 Output

Arrays

Arrays are a type of variable that has the power to store multiple values of the same data type and size. AutoIT allows you to store different data types in array, but it is not recommended because your performance will be decreased. It is always better to store the same data type in arrays. Declaring an array is the same as declaring a variable, but at the end you have to specify the number of elements you are going to store in the array by including the number inside the square bracket.

For e.g. Dim $vowels{5} ,Global $employeenames[6]

After declaring an array variable, you need to assign the value to your arrays by its index value. Index in array should always start with 0. Let's look at how to do that.

$vowels[0]="a"

$vowels[1]="e"

$vowels[2]="i"

$vowels[3]="o"

$vowels[4]="u"

To access the particular element, you need to specify its index. I need to display "o" in the message box. Let see how to do that.

Example 5.12

```
File Edit Search View Tools Options Language Buffers Help
 1    Dim $vowels[5]
 2    ;Assigning values to arrays
 3    $vowels[0]="a"
 4    $vowels[1]="e"
 5    $vowels[2]="i"
 6    $vowels[3]="o"
 7    $vowels[4]="u"
 8    ;Displaying the value of index 3
 9    MsgBox(0,"Vowels","The value stored in the index 3 is "&
10    $vowels[3])
```

Fig 5.21 Array Example

I declared an array variable $vowels of size 5 and assigned the value by specifying its index. Using the message box function, I'm trying to display the value stored in the index 3 i.e. "o." The output of the script is shown below:

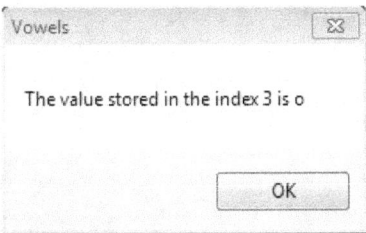

The value stored in the index 3 is o

OK

Fig 5.22 Output

You can also assign a value to the array variable while declaring as shown in example 5.13below:

Example 5.13

```
File Edit Search View Tools Options Language Buffers Help
1   ;Assigning values to arrays while declaring
2   Dim $vowels[5]=["a","e","i","o","u"]
3
4   ;Displaying the value of index 3
5   MsgBox(0,"Vowels","The value stored in the index 3 is "&
6   $vowels[3])
```

Fig 5.23 Array example

When you are declaring an array and assigning the value in the same statement, then the first element "a" takes the index 0 and it goes on in the ascending order. The output of the Ex 11 is same as example 10.

You can also declare a multi-dimensional array. Let's take a look at a two-dimensional array.

Two Dimensional Arrays

Two dimensional arrays are like rows and columns. Values in the first square bracket indicate the row and values in the second square bracket indicate columns.

For e.g. Dim $num[2][3]

Columns		
Rows	1	2	3
	4	5	6

Table 5.1

In table 5.1, we have two rows and three columns. I'm going to display the first element in the second row i.e. 4.

```
File  Edit  Search  View  Tools  Options  Language  Buffers  Help

 1    ;Declaring two dimensional arrays
 2    Dim $num[2][3]
 3
 4    ;Assigning values to 2D arrays
 5    $num[0][0] =1
 6    $num[0][1] =2
 7    $num[0][2] =3
 8    $num[1][0] =4
 9    $num[1][1] =5
10    $num[1][2] =6
11    ; Displaying value of $num[1][0]
12    MsgBox(0,"Vowels","The value stored in the"&
13    " $num[1][0] is "&$num[1][0])
```

Fig 5.24 Array Example

I initialized a two dimensional array in the first line and later on I assign the value to its corresponding rows and columns. Using the message box function, I'm trying to display $num[1][0] which lies in the second row and the first column. The output of the script is shown below:

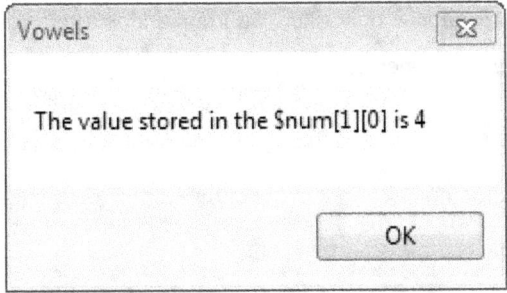

Fig 5.25 Output

6) Operators

Operators are sets of symbols used to perform various operations with operand and to return the result. AutoIT comes with the following types of operators:

1) Mathematical Operators

2) Assignment Operators

3) Concatenation Operators

4) Comparison Operators

5) Logical Operators

6) Conditional Operators

Let's look at each operator in detail.

1) Mathematical Operators

This Operator performs mathematical operations with its operands.

a) Addition Operator (+)

This operator adds one numeric value or variable to another numeric value or variable.

Syntax

Numeric Variable (or) Value+ Numeric Variable (or) Value

Parameters

Numeric Variable- Variable containing numbers

Numeric Value-Any numeric value

Example 6.1

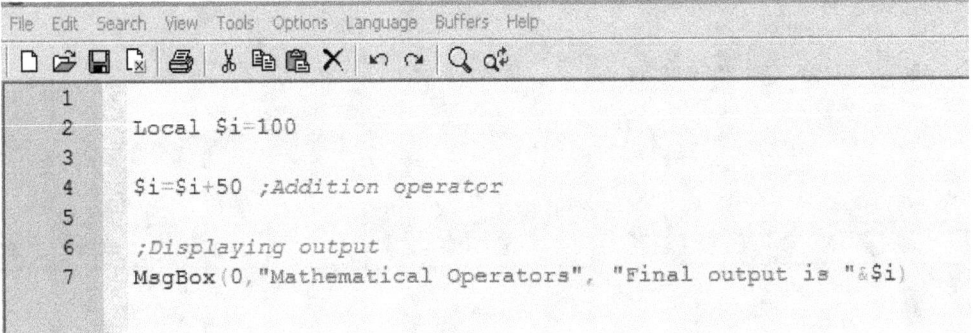

```
1
2       Local $i=100
3
4       $i=$i+50  ;Addition operator
5
6       ;Displaying output
7       MsgBox(0,"Mathematical Operators", "Final output is "&$i)
```

Fig 6.1 Addition Operator

In the above example, the Compiler adds variable $i having value 100 with numeric value 50 (which results in 150) and stores the final output in variable $i. The output of this operator is shown below:

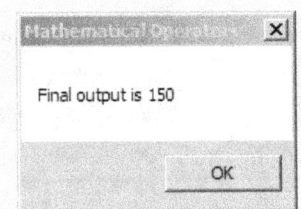

Fig 6.2 Output

Note: You cannot add string with string or numbers with string.

b) Subtraction Operator (-)

This operator subtracts one numeric value or variable from another numeric value or variable.

Syntax

Numeric Variable (or) Value - Numeric Variable (or) Value

Parameters

Numeric Variable- Variable containing numbers

Numeric Value-Any numeric value

Example 6.2

```
File  Edit  Search  View  Tools  Options  Language  Buffers  Help

1
2    Local $i=100
3
4    $i=$i-50 ;Subtraction operator
5
6    ;Displaying output
7    MsgBox(0,"Mathematical Operators", "Final output is "&$i)
```

Fig 6.3 Subtraction Operator

In the above example, the Compiler subtracts 50 from variable $i with value 100 and the final result is stored in the variable $i.

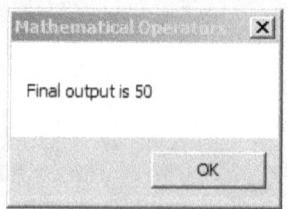

Final output is 50

OK

Fig 6.4 Output

Note: You cannot subtract string from string or numbers from string.

c) Multiplication Operator (*)

This operator multiplies one numeric value or variable with another numeric value or variable.

Syntax

Numeric Variable (or) Value * Numeric Variable (or) Value

Parameters

Numeric Variable- Variable containing numbers

Numeric Value-Any numeric value

Example 6.3

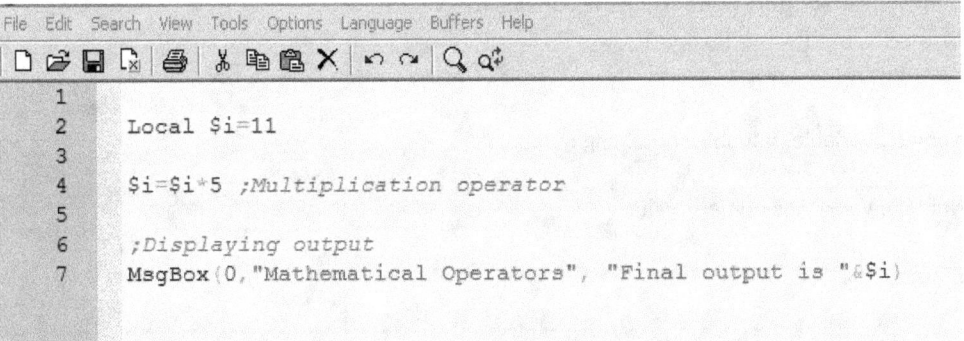

Fig 6.5 Multiplication Operator

The Multiplication operator multiplies the variable $i containing value 11 with value 5 and stores the final value to the variable $i.

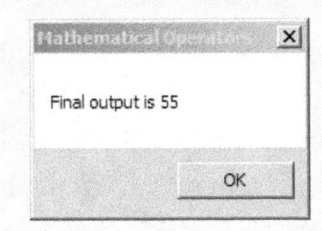

Fig 6.6 Output

Note: You cannot multiply string with string or numbers with string.

d) Division Operator (/)

This operator divides one numeric value or variable by another numeric value or variable.

Syntax

Numeric Variable (or) Value /Numeric Variable (or) Value

Parameters

Numeric Variable- Variable containing numbers

Numeric Value-Any numeric value

Example 6.4

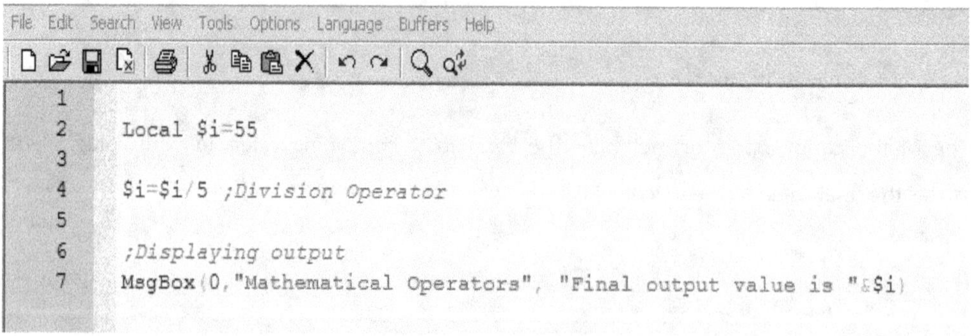

```
File Edit Search View Tools Options Language Buffers Help

1
2       Local $i=55
3
4       $i=$i/5 ;Division Operator
5
6       ;Displaying output
7       MsgBox(0,"Mathematical Operators", "Final output value is "&$i)
```

Fig 6.7 Division Operator

The Division operator divides the variable containing 55 by value 5 and stores the final value in the variable $i. Output is shown below:

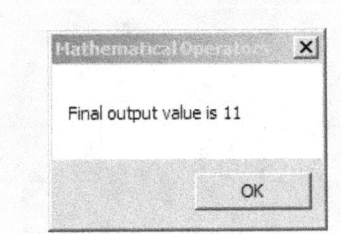

Final output value is 11

Fig 6.8 Output

Note: You cannot use this operator for a combination of string and numeric value or only string.

e) Exponentiation Operator (^)

This Operator raises a number or numeric variable to the power of another number or numeric variable.

Syntax

Numeric Variable (or) Value ^Numeric Variable (or) Value

Parameters

Numeric Variable- Variable containing numbers

Numeric Value-Any numeric value

Example 6.5

```
1
2      Local $i=5
3
4      Local $j=$i^3 ;Exponentiation Operator
5
6      ;Displaying output
7      MsgBox(0,"Mathematical Operators", "Final output value is "&$j)
```

Fig 6.9 Exponentiation operator

In the above example, the exponentiation operator raises the variable $i to the 3rd power and assigns the output to variable $j.

It can also be expressed as $j= $ i^ 3 = 5 ^ 3 = 5 * 5 * 5 = 125

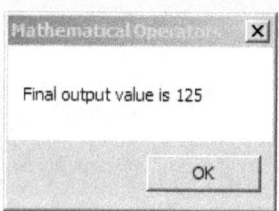

Final output value is 125

OK

Fig 6.10 Output

2) Assignment Operators

The Assignment Operator is used to get the value of the operand that exists to the right of the operator and assign it to the operand that exists to the left of it and perform operations depend upon the operator used. AutoIT contain five different types of assignment operators. They are:

a) Simple Assignment Operator (=)

This is one of the most commonly used operators in AutoIT. Simple assignment operator "=", assigns the exact value present on the right side of the operator to its left. In other words, it simply copies the right side operand's value and pastes it to the left side operand.

Syntax

Variable=Value

Parameters

Variable- Any type of variable

Value-It can be any alpha or numeric characters

Example 6.6

```
File  Edit  Search  View  Tools  Options  Language  Buffers  Help
1    Local $i
2
3    $i=20;Assignmet operator
4
5    ;Displaying the value of right side operand
6    MsgBox(0,"Assignment operator","The value assigned"&
7    "to its left side is "&$i)
```

Fig 6.11 Simple Assignment Operator

$i=20- Value 20 is present to the right of the operator and variable $i is present to the left of the operator. When the compiler detects the operator '=' then it assigns or copies the value 20 and pastes it to the variable $i. That's why it displays 20 when I use variable $i in the message box function.

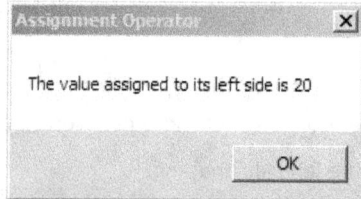

Fig 6.12 Output

Note: You can use this operator for string also.

b) Addition Assignment Operator (+=)

This adds a value to a variable and assigns the final result to the variable. It is used to increment the counter variable in Do..while and While..Wend loops.

Syntax

Variable+=Value

Parameter

Variable- Any numeric variable

Value- It can be any numeric expression

Example 6.7

```
File Edit Search View Tools Options Language Buffers Help
1    Local $i=15
2
3    $i+=20;Addition Assignmet operator
4
5    ;Displaying the value of right side operand
6    MsgBox(0,"Assignment operator","The value assigned"&
7    "to its left side is "&$i)
```

Fig 6.13 Addition assignment operator

Initially, the variable $i is declared and initialized with the value 15. The Addition assignment operator has been used to add 20 to the existing value.

$i+=20 It can also be expressed as $i=$i+20 which means $i=15+20=35.

So the final value 35 is assigned to variable $i and the same will be displayed in the message box function.

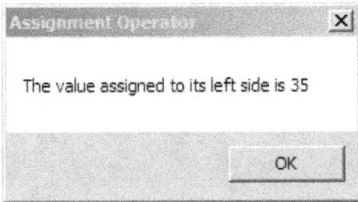

Fig 6.14 Output

What will happen if an expression is non-numeric?

The Addition assignment operator will work as you expect when value is numeric. When it is non- numeric then no action will be performed.

Example 6.8

```
File  Edit  Search  View  Tools  Options  Language  Buffers  Help
 1    Local $i=20
 2
 3    $i+="Hello";Addition Assignmet operator
 4
 5    ;Displaying the value of right side operand
 6    MsgBox(0,"Assignment operator","The value assigned"&
 7    "to its left side is "&$i)
```

Fig 6.15 Addition assignment Operator

Variable $i is declared and initialized with value 20 and I'm adding it to a string "Hello" and displaying the final result in the message box. But the final result displays the value 20. It neither concatenates string and number nor shows any error. It simply skips the addition assignment operation.

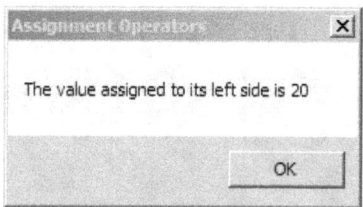

Fig 6.16 Output

c) Subtraction Assignment Operator (-=)

This subtracts a value from the variable and assigns the final result to the variable. It is used to decrement the counter variable in Do...While and While...Wend loop.

Syntax

Variable-=Value

Parameters

Variable- Any numeric variable

Value- It can be any numeric expression

Example 6.9

```
1    Local $i=40
2
3    $i-=20;Subtraction Assignmet operator
4
5    ;Displaying output
6    MsgBox(0,"Assignment operator","The value assigned"&
7    "to its left side is "&$i)
```

Fig 6.17 Subtraction assignment Operator

Declared and initialized a variable $i=40. The Subtraction assignment operator has been used to subtract 20 from 40.

$i-=20. It can also be expressed as $i=$i-20 which means $i=40-20=20

Finally the value 20 is assigned to a variable $i which exists to the right side of the operator and it is displayed in the message box.

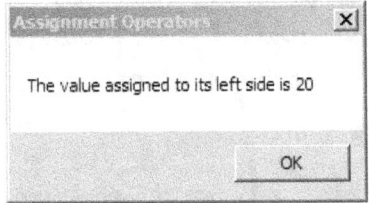

Fig 6.18 Output

Note: This operator should work only if the value is numeric. In the case of a non-numeric expression, it behaves in the same way as it behaves for Addition assignment operator.

d) Multiplication Assignment Operator (*=)

This multiplies a value to the variable and assigns the final result to the variable.

Syntax

Variable*=Value

Parameters

Variable- Any numeric variable

Value- It can be any numeric expression

Example 6.10

```
File Edit Search View Tools Options Language Buffers Help
1    Local $i=20
2
3    $i*=50;Multiplication Assignmet operator
4
5    ;Displaying output
6    MsgBox(0,"Assignment operator","The value assigned"&
7    "to its left side is "&$i)
```

Fig 6.19 Multiplication assignment operator

Declared and initialized a variable $i=20. The Multiplication assignment operator has been used to multiply 20 and 50.

$i*=50. It can also be expressed as $i=$i*50 which means $i=20*50=100

Finally the value 1000 is assigned to a variable $i which exists to the right side of the operator and the same will be displayed in the message box.

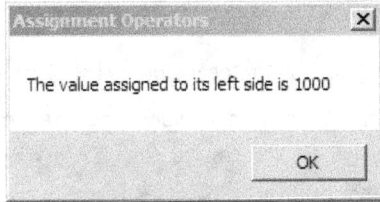

Fig 6.20 Output

Note: This operator should work only if the value is numeric. In the case of a non-numeric expression, it behaves in the same way as it behaves for Addition assignment operator.

e) Division Assignment Operator (/*)

This divides the variable by a value and assigns the final result to the variable.

Syntax

Variable/=Value

Parameters

Variable- Any numeric variable

Value- It can be any numeric expression

Example 6.11

```
File Edit Search View Tools Options Language Buffers Help

1    Local $i=100
2
3    $i/=50;Division Assignmet operator
4
5    ;Displaying output
6    MsgBox(0,"Assignment operator","The value assigned"& _
7    "to its left side is "&$i)
```

Fig 6.21 Division assignment operator

I declared and initialized a local variable $i with value 100. With the help of the division assignment operator I am able to divide the variable by the given numeric value and alter the value of local variable $i.

$i/=50- It can also be expressed as $i=$i/50 which means 100/50=2

Finally the local variable $i is altered to value 2 and the same is displayed in the message box.

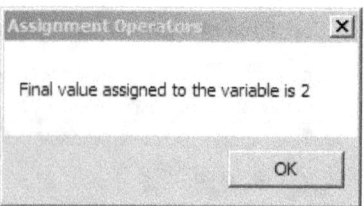

Fig 6.22 Output

3) Concatenation Operators

This is used to combine or concatenate characters in the string end to end.

a) Simple ConcatenationOperator (&)

This is used to concatenate one string or string variable with another string or string variable. It can concatenate digits, alphabetic characters and special characters. This operator simply combines the string and it won't perform any arithmetic operations between strings.

Syntax

String Variable (or) String & String Variable (or) String

Parameters

String variable= It denotes that the variable contains strings such as alphabetical characters, digits and punctuations.

String – It denotes that the string contains alphabetical characters, digits and punctuations.

Example 6.12

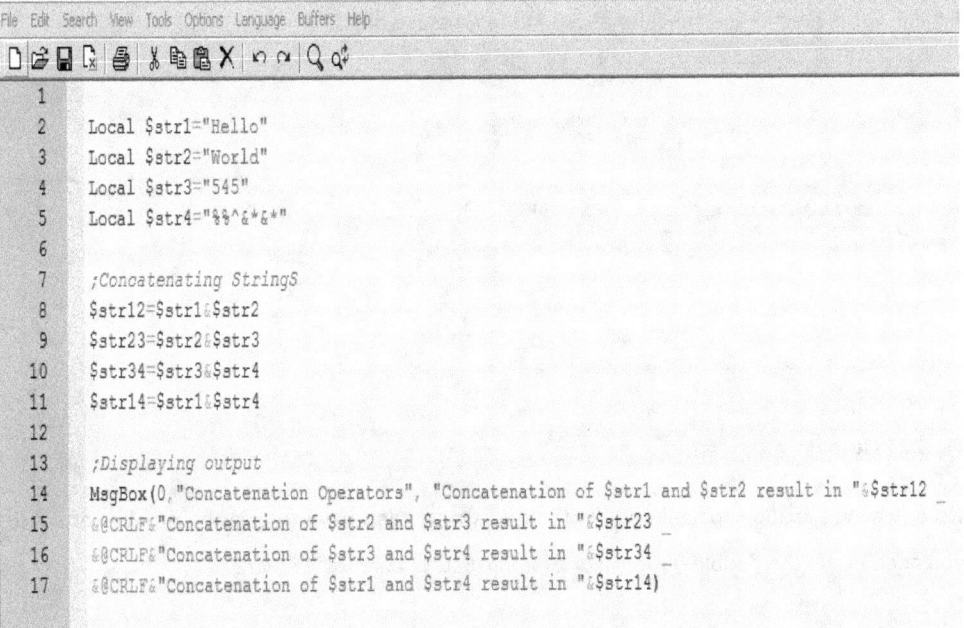

```
File  Edit  Search  View  Tools  Options  Language  Buffers  Help

1
2      Local $str1="Hello"
3      Local $str2="World"
4      Local $str3="545"
5      Local $str4="%%^&*&*"
6
7      ;Concatenating StringS
8      $str12=$str1&$str2
9      $str23=$str2&$str3
10     $str34=$str3&$str4
11     $str14=$str1&$str4
12
13     ;Displaying output
14     MsgBox(0,"Concatenation Operators", "Concatenation of $str1 and $str2 result in "&$str12
15     &@CRLF&"Concatenation of $str2 and $str3 result in "&$str23
16     &@CRLF&"Concatenation of $str3 and $str4 result in "&$str34
17     &@CRLF&"Concatenation of $str1 and $str4 result in "&$str14)
```

Fig 6.23 Simple Concatenation operator

In the above example, I declared and initialized 4 strings "Hello," "World," "545" & "%%^&*&*" and assigned them to variables $str1, $str2, $str3 and $str4 respectively. Now I'm going to combine two different strings in multiple combinations.

$str12=$str1&$str2-This statement concatenates the strings "Hello" and "World" and assigns them to variable $str12

$str23=$str2&$str3-This statement concatenates the strings "World" and numbers "545" and assigns them to variable $str23

$str34=$str3&$str4-This statement concatenates the numbers "545" and special characters "%%^&*&*" and assigns them to variable $str34

$str14=$str1&$str4-This statement concatenates the strings "Hello" and special characters "%%^&*&*" and assigns them to variable $str14

Finally, I displayed all the concatenations in the message box:

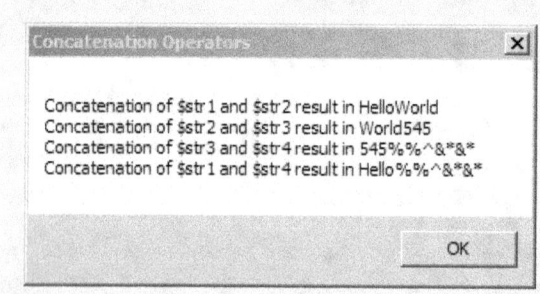

Fig 6.24 Output

Note: It won't include space between the two strings. You have to give the number of spaces you need inside the double quotes. For example $str12=$str1& " "&$str2.

b) Concatenation Assignment Operator (&=)

This concatenates string to string variables and assigns the concatenated strings to a variable.

Syntax

String Variable &= String

Parameters

String variable= It denotes the variable containing strings such as alphabetic characters, digits and punctuations.

String – It denote the string containing alphabetic characters, digits and punctuations.

Example 6.13

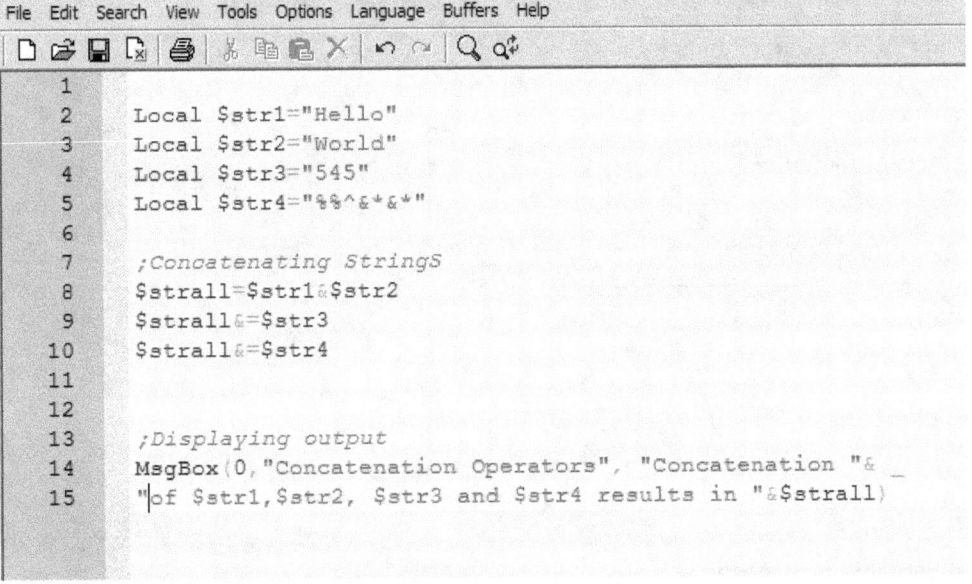

```
1
2       Local $str1="Hello"
3       Local $str2="World"
4       Local $str3="545"
5       Local $str4="%%^&*&*"
6
7       ;Concatenating Strings
8       $strall=$str1&$str2
9       $strall&=$str3
10      $strall&=$str4
11
12
13      ;Displaying output
14      MsgBox(0,"Concatenation Operators", "Concatenation "& _
15      "of $str1,$str2, $str3 and $str4 results in "&$strall)
```

Fig 6.25 Concatenation assignment Operator

Using the concatenation assignment operator, I'm trying to combine the string $str1, $str2, $str3 and $str4 and assign the concatenated string to variable $strall.

$strall=$str1&$str2 – This statement performs a simple concatenation operation which combines "Hello" and "World" and results in "HelloWorld" and assigns it to the variable $strall.

$strall&=$str3- This statement concatenates $strall with $str3 and stores the concatenated string to $strall. In other words, it combines "HelloWorld and "545," which results in "HelloWorld545" and stores it again to $strall

$strall&=$str4- This statement concatenates $strall with $str4 and stores the concatenated string again to $strall. Before this statement performs, the variable $strall contains the string "HelloWorld545." This statement concatenates "HelloWorld545" and "%%^&*&*" and makes it "HelloWorld545%%^&*&*."

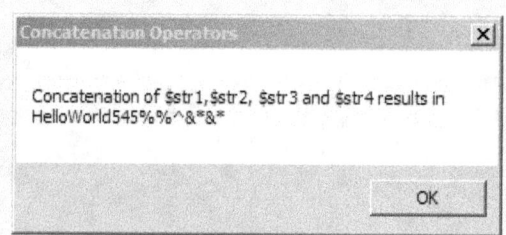

Fig 6.26 Output

4) Comparison Operators

This is used to compare two values and return true or false.

a) Equivalence Operator

This operator compares the two operands and returns true only if they are identical to each other (i.e. both letters and cases must be identical.) It converts the operand to a string first and starts comparing. It assumes characters, letters and symbols as strings and performs the operation.

Syntax

Expression1 == Expression2

Parameters

Expression1- It denotes any expression

Expression2- It denotes any expression

Example 6.14

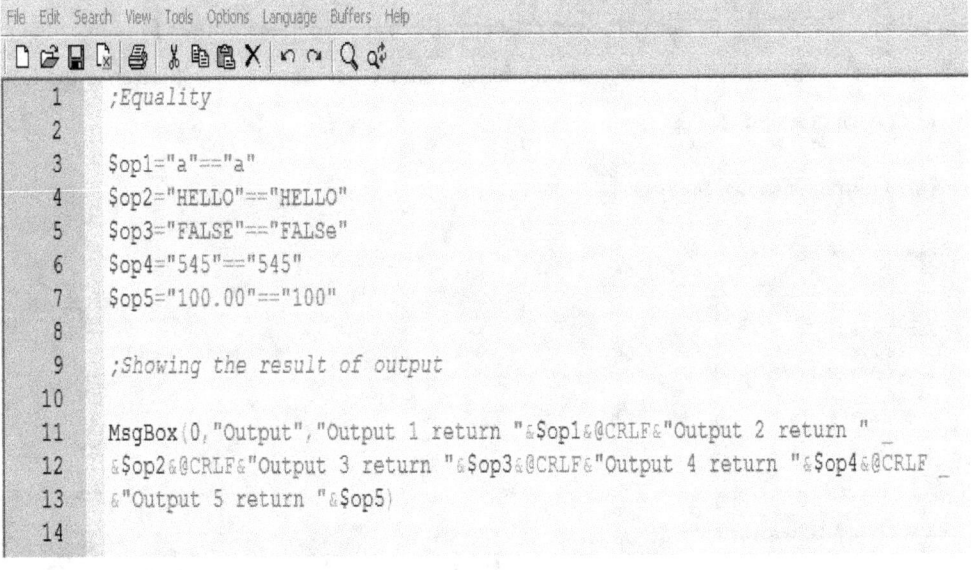

```
File  Edit  Search  View  Tools  Options  Language  Buffers  Help
    1      ;Equality
    2
    3      $op1="a"=="a"
    4      $op2="HELLO"=="HELLO"
    5      $op3="FALSE"=="FALSe"
    6      $op4="545"=="545"
    7      $op5="100.00"=="100"
    8
    9      ;Showing the result of output
   10
   11      MsgBox(0,"Output","Output 1 return "&$op1&@CRLF&"Output 2 return " _
   12      &$op2&@CRLF&"Output 3 return "&$op3&@CRLF&"Output 4 return "&$op4&@CRLF _
   13      &"Output 5 return "&$op5)
   14
```

Fig 6.27 Equivalence operator

$op1

Statement "a"=="a" returns true because both letters and cases match with each other

$op2

Statement "HELLO"=="HELLO" return true because here also both letters and cases match with each other

$op3

Statement "FALSE"=="FALSe" return false because the last letter of the operand 2 fails to match with the last letter of operand 1

$op4

Statement "545"=="545" returns true because both numbers match with each other

$op5

Statement "100.00"=="100" is mathematically equal, but this operator returns false because it won't perform any arithmetic operations. Instead, it simple compares the first letter to the last letter of each operand.

The final output is shown below:

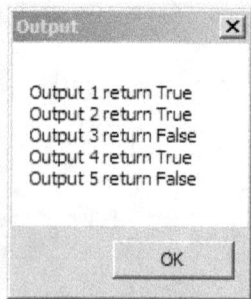

Fig 6.28 Output

b) Not Equal to Operator

This works in the reverse way of equal to operator. It performs a comparison and returns true if the operands are not equal to each other and returns false if they are equal to each other. It is case insensitive. It performs arithmetic operations. To perform an unequal case sensitive comparison, you have to use a combination of NOT and "==" operators.

Syntax

Expression1 <> Expression2

Parameters

Expression1- It denotes any expression

Expression2- It denotes any expression

Example 6.15

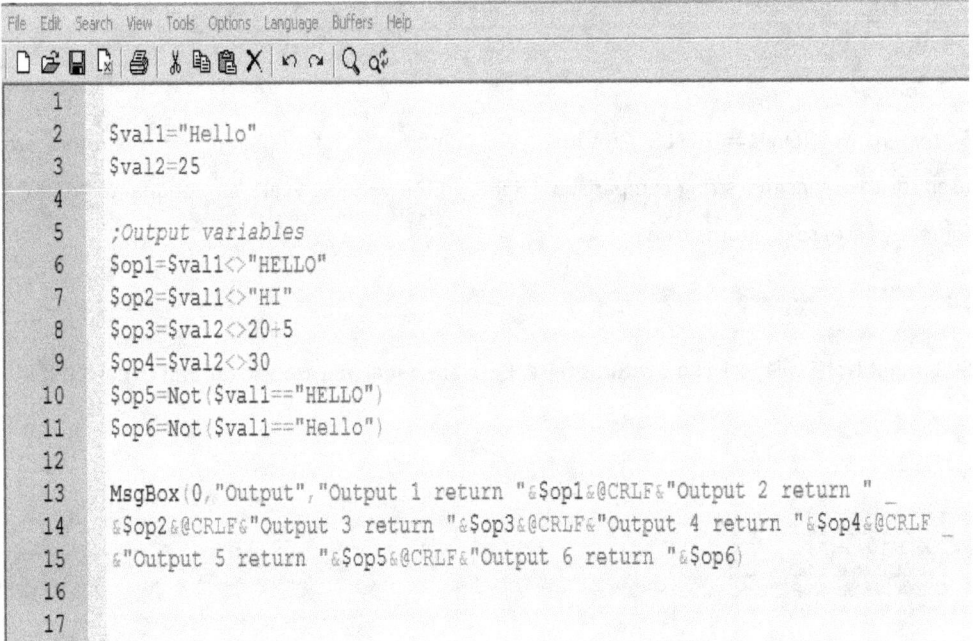

```
 1
 2     $val1="Hello"
 3     $val2=25
 4
 5     ;Output variables
 6     $op1=$val1<>"HELLO"
 7     $op2=$val1<>"HI"
 8     $op3=$val2<>20+5
 9     $op4=$val2<>30
10     $op5=Not($val1=="HELLO")
11     $op6=Not($val1=="Hello")
12
13     MsgBox(0,"Output","Output 1 return "&$op1&@CRLF&"Output 2 return " _
14     &$op2&@CRLF&"Output 3 return "&$op3&@CRLF&"Output 4 return "&$op4&@CRLF _
15     &"Output 5 return "&$op5&@CRLF&"Output 6 return "&$op6)
16
17
```

Fig 6.29 Not equal to operator

$op1

Statement $val1<>"HELLO" returns false because both "Hello" assigned to variable $var1 and "HELLO" are equal (<> is Case- insensitive)

$op2

Statement $val1<>"HI" returns true because both "Hello" and "HI" are different.

$op3

Statement $val2<>20+5 returns false. As I mentioned previously, it allows mathematical operations so it adds 20 &5and compares it with $val2 which contains the value 25. Both are equal so it returns false.

$op4

Statement $val2<>30 returns true because 25 stored in the $val2 is not equal to 30.

$op5

Statement Not ($val1=="HELLO") returns true. Combination of NOT and "==" operators are used for case sensitive string comparison. "Hello" in the variable $val1 is not equal to "HELLO" (differ by case) so it returns true.

$op6

Statement Not($val1=="Hello") returns false. Both are equal (in case and letters) to each other.

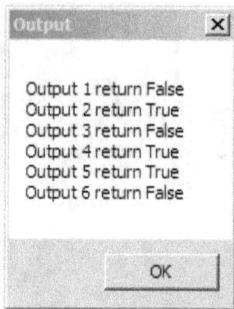

Fig 6.30 Output

c) Greater than operator

This operator compares both operands and returns true if the left operand is greater than the right operand. It returns false if the left operand is equal to or lesser than the right operand.

Syntax

Expression1 >Expression2

Parameters

Expression1- It denotes any numeric expression

Expression2- It denotes any numeric expression

Example 6.16

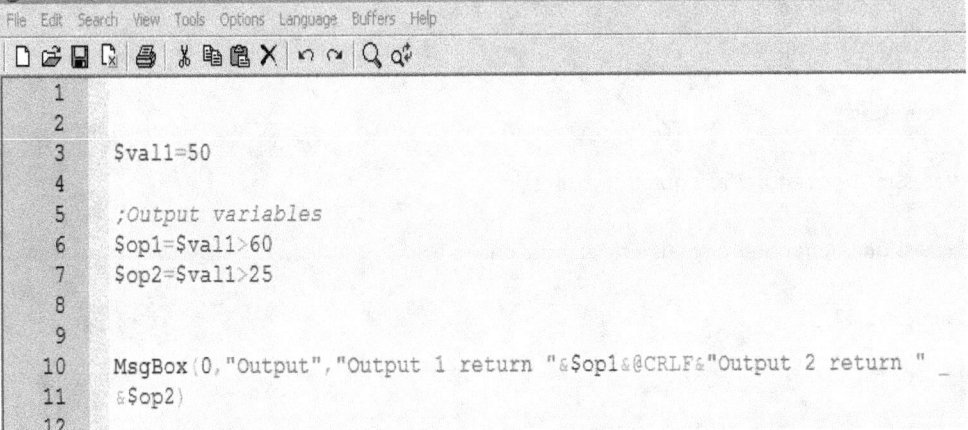

Fig 6.31 Greater than operator

$op1

Statement $val1>60 returns false because 50 is not greater than 60.

$op2

Statement $val1>25 returns true because 50 is greater than 25

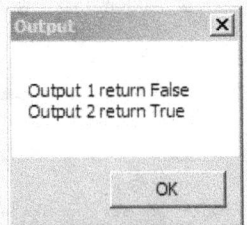

Fig 6.32 Output

d) Greater than or equal to Operator

This operator compares both operands and returns true if the left operand is greater than or equal to the right operand. It returns false if the left operand is lesser than the right operand.

Syntax

Expression1 >= Expression2

Parameters

Expression1- It denotes any numeric expression

Expression2- It denotes any numeric expression

Example 6.17

```
1
2
3     $val1=50
4
5     ;Output variables
6     $op1=$val1>=45
7     $op2=$val1>=50
8     $op3=$val1>=55
9
10
11    MsgBox(0,"Output","Output 1 return "&$op1&@CRLF&"Output 2 return "
12    &$op2&@CRLF&"Output 3 return "&$op3 )
13
```

Fig 6.33 Greater than or equal to operator

$op1

Statement $val1>=45 returns true because 50 is greater than 45

$op2

Statement $val1>=50 returns true because 50 is equal to 50

$op3

Statement $val1>=55 returns false because 50 is not greater than 55

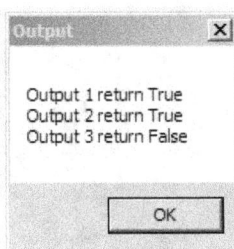

Output 1 return True
Output 2 return True
Output 3 return False

Fig 6.34 Output

e) Lesser than operator

This operator compares both operands and returns true if the left operand is lesser than the right operand. It returns false if the left operand is greater than or equal to the right operand.

Syntax

Expression1 <Expression2

Parameters

Expression1- It denotes any numeric expression

Expression2- It denotes any numeric expression

Example 6.18

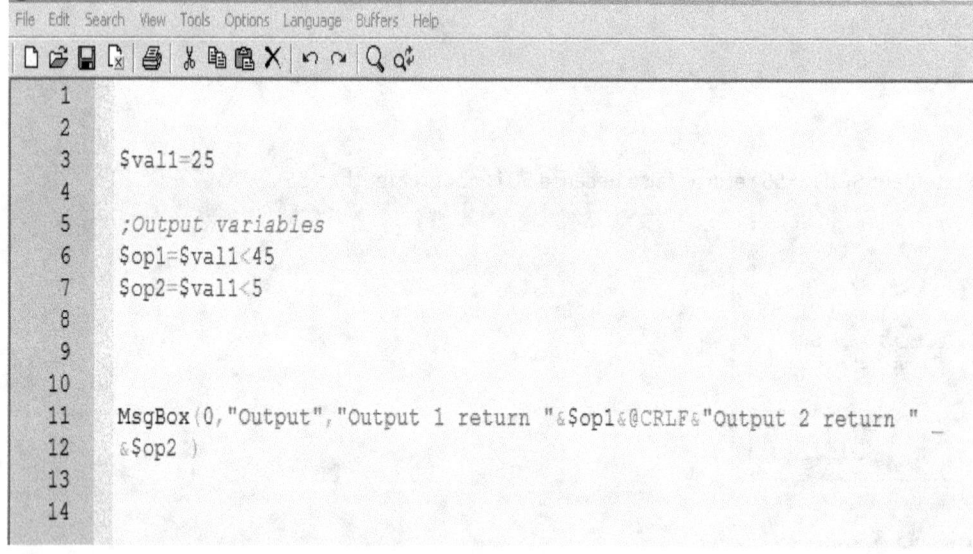

```
File Edit Search View Tools Options Language Buffers Help

 1
 2
 3     $val1=25
 4
 5     ;Output variables
 6     $op1=$val1<45
 7     $op2=$val1<5
 8
 9
10
11     MsgBox(0,"Output","Output 1 return "&$op1&@CRLF&"Output 2 return " _
12     &$op2 )
13
14
```

Fig 6.35 Lesser than operator

Statement returns true because variable $val1 having value 25 is lesser than 45 and $val1<5 returns false because 25 is not lesser than 5.

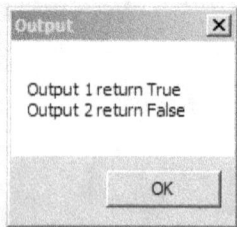

Output 1 return True
Output 2 return False

OK

Fig 6.36 Output

f) Lesser than or equal to Operator

This operator compares both operands and returns true if the left operand is lesser than or equal to the right operand. It returns false if the left operand is greater than the right operand.

Syntax

Expression1 <= Expression2

Parameters

Expression1- It denotes any numeric expression

Expression2- It denotes any numeric expression

Example 6.19

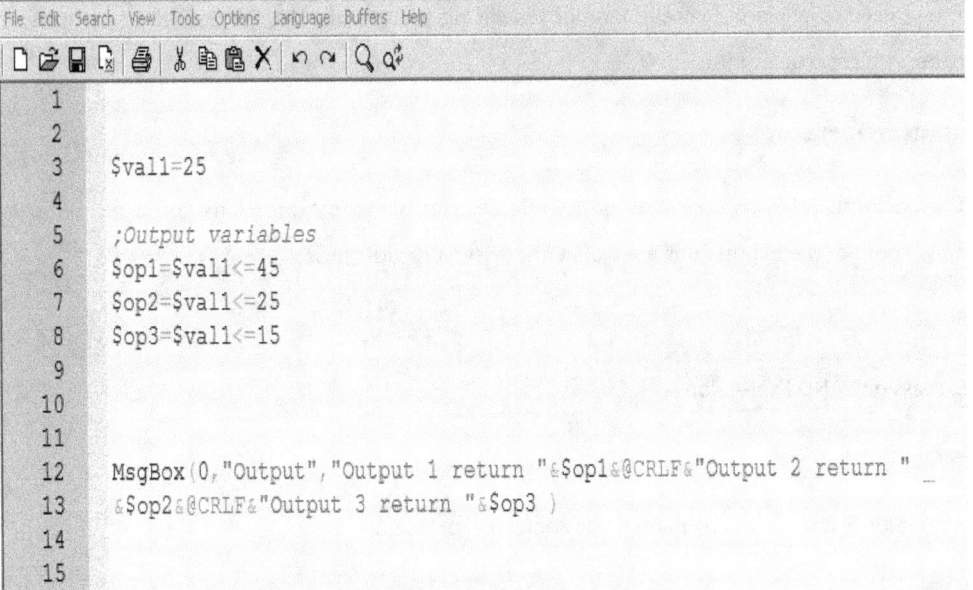

Fig 6.37 Lesser than or equal to operator

Statement $val1<=45 returns true because 25 is lesser than 45, $val1<=25 returns true because 25 is equal to 25 and $val1<=15 returns false because 25 is not lesser than 15

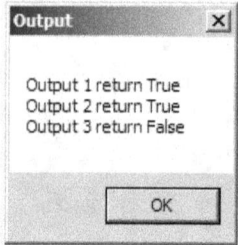

Fig 6.38 Output

5) Logical Operators

This is used to perform logical operations involving the use of AND, OR and NOT operators. It either returns true or false.

a) AND Operator

This performs a logical operation on two Boolean or numeric expressions and it returns true only if both of the expressions are true. Otherwise, it returns false.

Syntax

Expression1 AND Expression2

Parameters

Expression1- It denotes any numeric or Boolean expression

Expression2- It denotes any numeric or Boolean expression

S.No	Expression 1	Expresion 2	Output
1	TRUE	TRUE	TRUE
2	FALSE	TRUE	FALSE
3	TRUE	FALSE	FALSE
4	FALSE	FALSE	FALSE

Table 6.1 Truth Table for AND Operator

Example 6.20

File Edit Search View Tools Options Language Buffers Help

```
1   ;Variable 1 and 2
2   Local $val1=20
3   Local $val2=45
4
5   ;Output 1 and 2
6   Local $op1=$val1>10 And $val2<50
7   Local $op2=$val1<15 And $val2>35
8
9   ;Showing the result of two outputs
10  MsgBox(0,"Output"," Output 1 return "&$op1&@CRLF&" Output 2 return "&$op2)
11
12
```

Fig 6.39 AND Operator

Two variables $val1 and $val2 are declared and initialized with the values 20 and 45 respectively. To understand the working of AND operator, I've created two local variables $op1 and $op2.

In the $op1, two comparisons are combined with AND Operator. First comparison $val1>10 is true because 20 is greater than 10 and second comparison $val2<50 is also true because 45 is less than 50. AND operator in the $op1 returns true because both the expressions return true.

In $op2 variable, one comparison is true ($val2>35) and other one is false ($val1<15) so AND operator returns false. Output of $op1 and $op2 is shown below

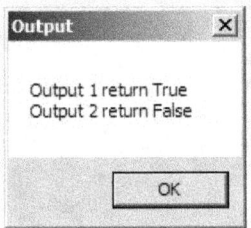

Fig 6.40 Output

b) OR Operator

This performs a logical operation on two Boolean or numeric expressions and returns true if both or any one of the expression is true. It returns false only if both the expressions are false.

Syntax

Expression1 OR Expression2

Parameters

Expression1- It denotes any numeric or Boolean expression

Expression2- It denotes any numeric or Boolean expression

S.No	Expression 1	Expresion 2	Output
1	TRUE	TRUE	TRUE
2	FALSE	TRUE	TRUE
3	TRUE	FALSE	TRUE
4	FALSE	FALSE	FALSE

Table 6.2Truth Table for OR operator

Example 6.21

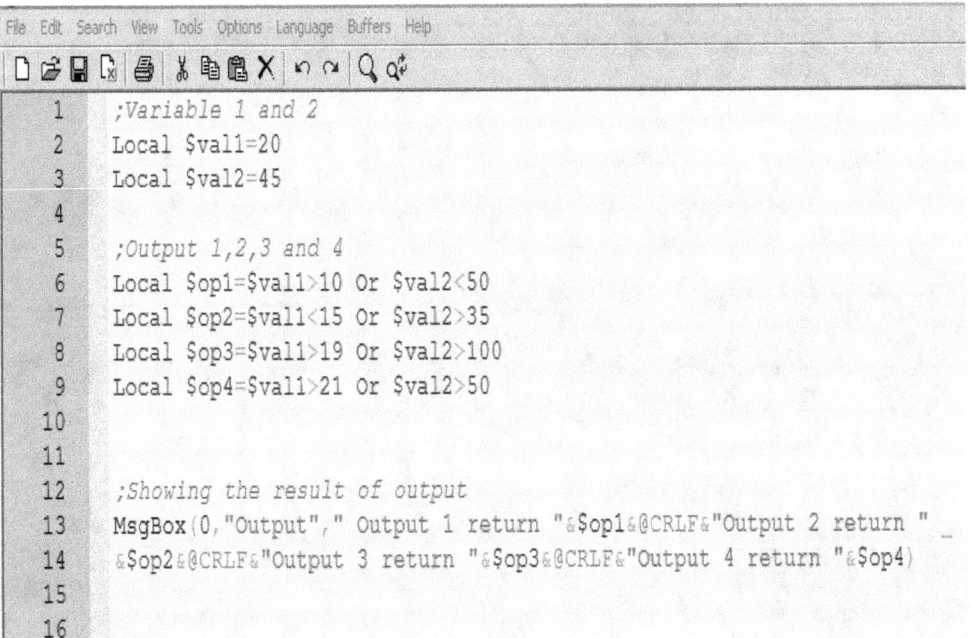

Fig 6.41 OR operator

$op1

Expressions $val1>10 returns true and $val2<50 also returns true. Since both expressions return true, S.No 1 in the truth table means the OR operator returns true.

$op2

Expressions $val1<15 returns false and $val2>35 returns true so the OR operator also returns true as per S.No 2 in the truth table.

$op3

Expression $val1>19 returns true and $val2>100 returns false so the OR operator returns true as per S.No 3 in the truth table.

$op4

Expression $val1>21 returns false and $val2>50 also returns false so the OR operator returns false as per S.No 4 in the truth table.

Final output is shown in the message box:

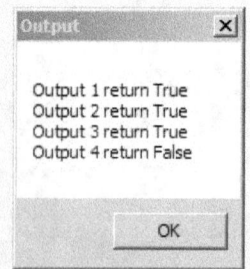

Fig 6.42 Output

c) NOT Operator

This performs a logical operation on a Boolean or numeric expression and it returns true if an expression is false and returns false if an expression is true.

Syntax

NOT Expression1

Parameters

Expression1- It denotes any numeric or Boolean expression

S.No	Expression 1	Output
1	TRUE	FALSE
2	FALSE	TRUE

Table 6.3 Truth Table for NOT operator

Example 6.22

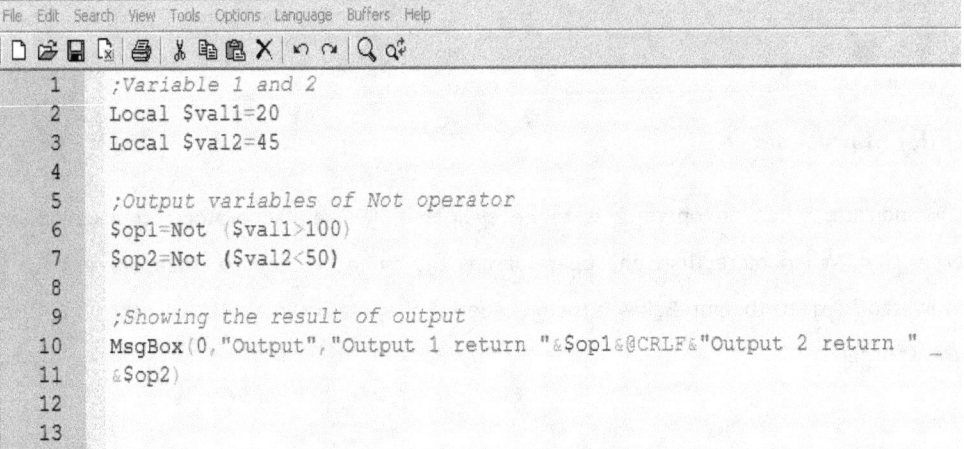

```
 1    ;Variable 1 and 2
 2    Local $val1=20
 3    Local $val2=45
 4
 5    ;Output variables of Not operator
 6    $op1=Not ($val1>100)
 7    $op2=Not ($val2<50)
 8
 9    ;Showing the result of output
10    MsgBox(0,"Output","Output 1 return "&$op1&@CRLF&"Output 2 return " _
11    &$op2)
12
13
```

Fig 6.43 NOT operator

$op1

$val1 >100 which means 20 is greater than 100. We all know that this is definitely false, but the NOT operator returns true.

$op2

$val2<50 indicates that 45 is less than 50. Of course this is true, but the NOT operator converts it into false and assigns value to $op2.

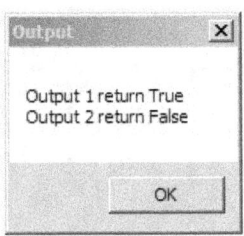

Fig 6.44 Output

Order of precedence

This indicates when an operator is to be evaluated if several operators are used in an expression. When more than one operator has the same precedence, then operators are evaluated from left to right. Below is the precedence of operators in AutoIT from the highest to lowest order.

Not

^

* ,/

+ , -

&

< ,>,<=, >=, =, <>,==

And, Or

If an expression is defined within angular bracket "() "then the expression within it will be evaluated first.

Example 6.23

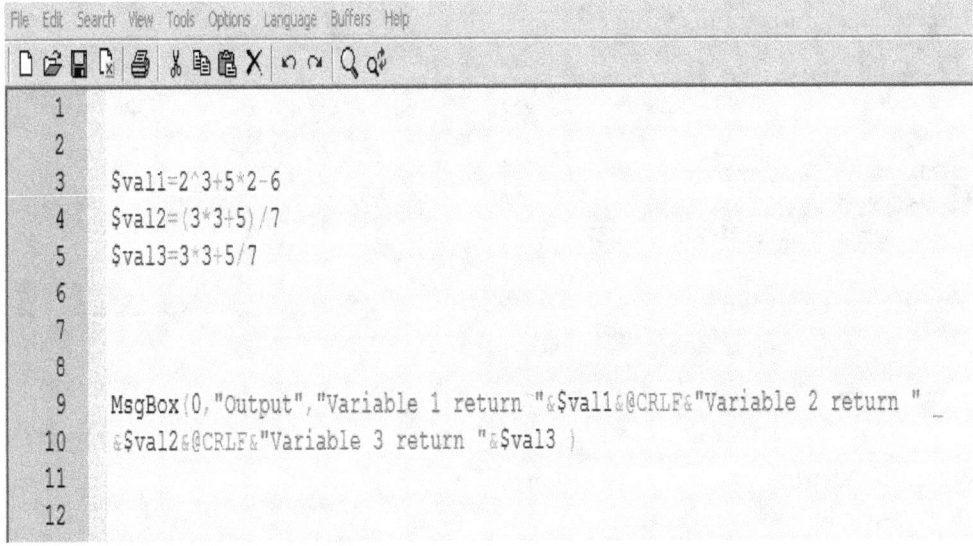

Fig 6.45 Order of precedence

$val1

This variable contains 2^3+5*2 – 6. Let's pick only the operators present in the statement ^ + * - . Now arrange it in the order of precedence i.e. ^ * + -.First precedence goes to ^ so it should be evaluated first, (2^3 results in 8). Second precedence goes to Operator * so it should be evaluated next, (5 *2 result is 10). Third precedence goes to + so it adds 8 & 10 which results in 18. Fourth precedence goes to – which results in 18-6 =12.

$val2

This variable contains (3*3+5)/7. The order of precedence of the operators used in the variable is (),* ,/, +. First precedence goes to parenthesis so expressions within it should be evaluated first. (3*3+5). Within the parenthesis, first precedence goes to * so 3*3 which results in 9 is addedto 5 , which equals 14. Then finally it is divided by 7 which results in 2.

$val3

Try it yourself. The result will be 9.71428

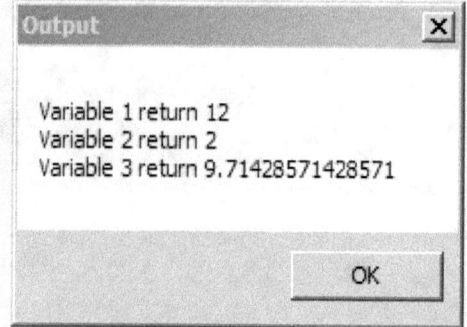

Fig 6.46 Output

7) Selection statements

AutoIT supports three selection statements: if, switch and select. This statement controls the flow of your program's execution based on the condition matches at the run time. We will look at each type of selection statements in detail with examples.

If...Then statement

The if statement ensures the condition given by the programmer is true. If the condition is true thenthe if statement will execute. Otherwise, the compiler will skip the statement and start compiling the next statement. It is a single line selection statement.

Syntax

If **<condition>** then **<instructions>**

Example 7.1

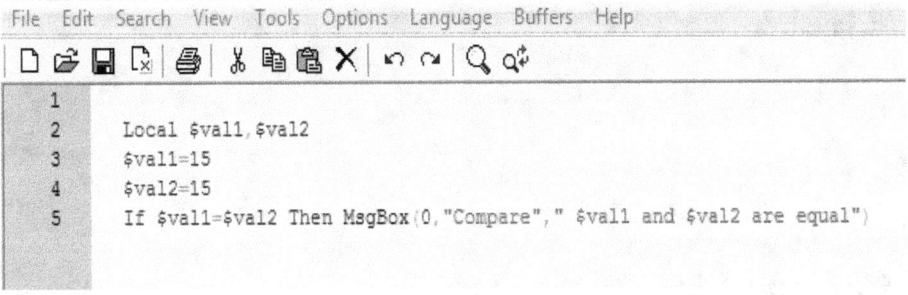

Fig 7.1 If statement

In the above example I initialized two variables $val1 and $val2 in the first statement. In the next two lines I assigned value 15 to those two variables. With the help of the If...Then statement I'm comparing the values of the variable $val1 and $val2 and when the condition is satisfied it displays the message box function as shown below. When the condition fails then the compiler starts compiling the next statement (If any).

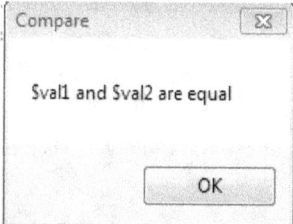

Fig 7.2 Output

If your instruction(s) is large or if you feel that it will be better if you place your instructions in the next line then, you can very well do that.However, ensure that you close it with the EndIf statement.

Syntax

If **<condition>** then

      <instructions>

      <Instructions>

EndIf

Example 7.2

```
File  Edit  Search  View  Tools  Options  Language  Buffers  Help

1
2      Local $val1,$val2
3      $val1=15
4      $val2=15
5    ⊟ If $val1=$val2 Then
6        MsgBox(0,"Compare"," $val1 and $val2 are equal")
7    └ EndIf
```

Fig 7.3 If statement

In the above example, I move the msgbox function to the next line so I need to close the If statement with EndIf keyword, but the Output of this script is the same as the previous example.

If... Else Statement

The instruction given in the If statement will be executed only if the condition is true and for all other cases the instruction given in the else statement will be executed.

Syntax

If <condition> then

<instructions>

Else

<Instructions>

EndIf

Example 7.3

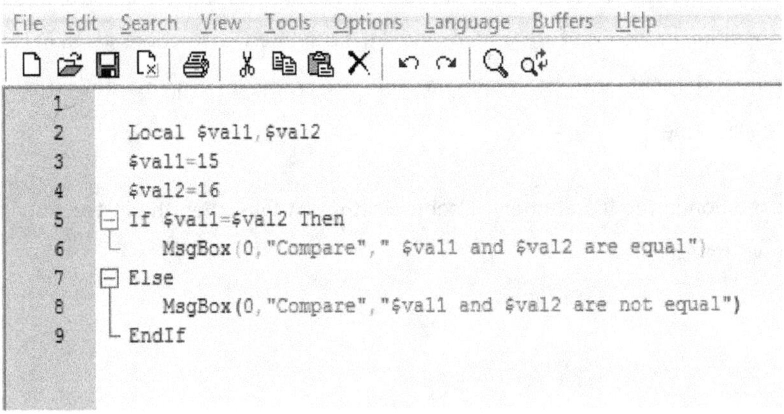

Fig 7.4 If...Else statement

In the above example, I altered the value of variable $val2 to 16. When the If condition checks for the equality, it will fail, so the instruction inside the If statement will not be executed and the compiler will skip the instruction of the If statement and start compiling the Else statement instructions. In our case, $val1 and $val2 are not equal, so the msgbox function in the Else statement will be executed as shown below

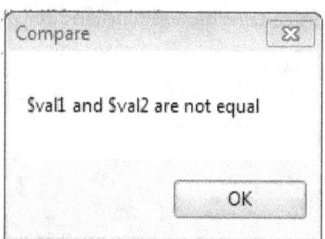

Fig 7.5 Output

If...ElseIf...Else...EndIf

The Compiler compiles the If...ElseIf...Else...EndIf statement in ascending order, which means it first checks the condition in the If statement and if it's true then instructions given in the If statement will be executed. Then, the compiler comes out of If...ElseIf...Else...EndIf statement.

Else, it checks the condition in the ElseIf statement, and if it's true then instructions given in the corresponding ElseIf statement will be executed and the compiler comes out of the If...ElseIf...Else...EndIf statement.

Finally, when the condition in the If statement, ElseIf(s) Statement fails, then the instruction in the Else statement will be executed.

Syntax

If **<condition>** then

        <Instructions>

Elseif**<condition>** then

    <Instructions>

Elseif**<condition>**then

    <Instructions>

....

Else **<Instruction>** then

End If

Example 7.4

```
File   Edit   Search   View   Tools   Options   Language   Buffers   Help

 1
 2        Local $val1,$val2
 3        $val1=15
 4        $val2=16
 5
 6        ;If...ElseIf...Else...EndIf Example
 7
 8     ┌ If $val1=$val2 Then
 9     └     MsgBox(0,"Compare"," $val1 and $val2 are equal")
10     ┌ ElseIf $val1>$val2 Then
11     └     MsgBox(0,"Compare"," $val1 is greater than $val2")
12     ┌ ElseIf $val1<$val2 Then
13     └     MsgBox(0,"Compare","$val1 is lesser than $val2")
14     ┌ Else
15     │     MsgBox(0,"Compare","Unable to compare")
16     └ EndIf
```

Fig 7.6 If...ElseIf...Else...EndIf statement

In the above example, the condition given in the If statement checks whether the $val1 and $val2 are equal, and if it's true then it displays the message '$val1 and $val2 are equal." Otherwise the compiler skips to the next ElseIf statement.

The first ElseIf statement checks whether $val1 is greater than $val2, and if it's true then it displays the message "$val1 is greater than $val2." Otherwise the compiler skips to the next ElseIf statement.

The second ElseIf statement checks whether $val1 is lesser than $val2, and if it's true then it displays the message "$val1 is lesser than $val2." Otherwise the compiler skips to the next Else statement.

When none of the above conditions are true, then by default instructions given in the Else statement will be executed. If there is no final Else statement and all other conditions are failed, then no action will be taken.

In our case, 15 are lesser than 16, so the condition given in the second ElseIf statement is true and its corresponding instructions will be executed.

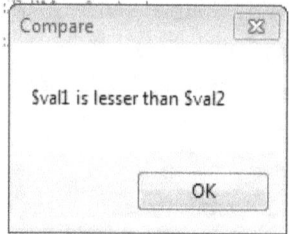

Fig 7.7 Output

Nested If statement

AutoIT supports Nested If statements. This statement contains If..Else statements inside other If..Else statements.

When the condition in the If statement is true and the condition in the Nested if statement is true, then the If..Else statement nested to the If statement will start compiling and its instruction will be executed. The same rule is applicable to Nested If..Else statements in the ElseIf and Else statement.

Syntax

If **<condition>** then

    <Instructions>

    If <**Condition**>then

        <Instructions>

    Endif

Elseif**<condition>** then

    <Instructions>

    If **<Condition>** then

        <instructions>

    Elself**<Condition>** then

        <instructions>

    Endlf

Elseif**<condition>**then

    If **<Condition>** then

ElseIf<**Condition**> then

<instructions>

EndIf

....

Else <**Instruction**> then

If <**Condition**> then

<instructions>

ElseIf<**Conditon**>Then

<instructions>

Else

<Instructions>

End If

Example 7.5

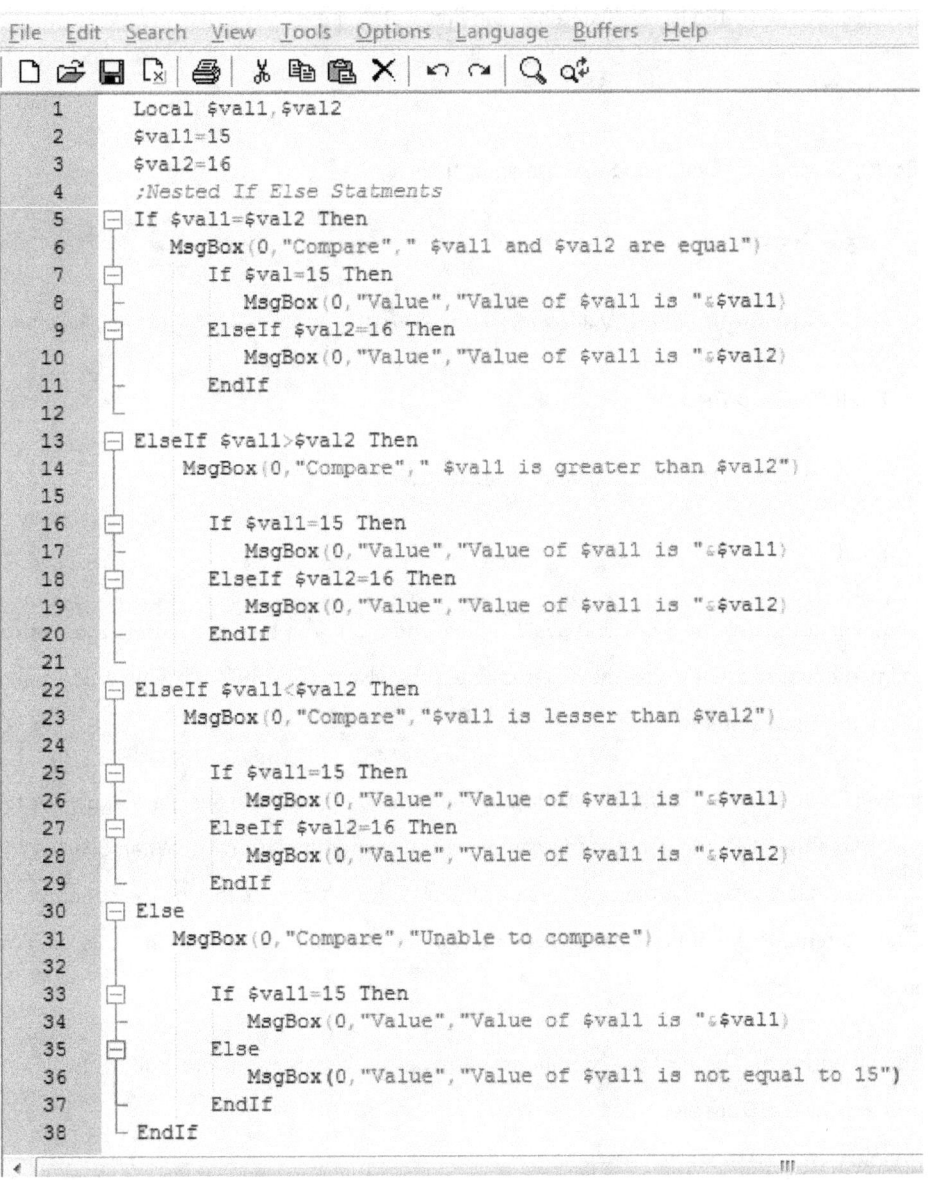

```
 1      Local $val1,$val2
 2      $val1=15
 3      $val2=16
 4      ;Nested If Else Statments
 5   ┌─ If $val1=$val2 Then
 6   │      MsgBox(0,"Compare"," $val1 and $val2 are equal")
 7   │  ┌─    If $val=15 Then
 8   │  ├─        MsgBox(0,"Value","Value of $val1 is "&$val1)
 9   │  ┌─    ElseIf $val2=16 Then
10   │  │         MsgBox(0,"Value","Value of $val1 is "&$val2)
11   │  ├─    EndIf
12   │  └
13   ┌─ ElseIf $val1>$val2 Then
14   │      MsgBox(0,"Compare"," $val1 is greater than $val2")
15   │
16   │  ┌─    If $val1=15 Then
17   │  ├─        MsgBox(0,"Value","Value of $val1 is "&$val1)
18   │  ┌─    ElseIf $val2=16 Then
19   │  │         MsgBox(0,"Value","Value of $val1 is "&$val2)
20   │  ├─    EndIf
21   │  └
22   ┌─ ElseIf $val1<$val2 Then
23   │      MsgBox(0,"Compare","$val1 is lesser than $val2")
24   │
25   │  ┌─    If $val1=15 Then
26   │  ├─        MsgBox(0,"Value","Value of $val1 is "&$val1)
27   │  ┌─    ElseIf $val2=16 Then
28   │  │         MsgBox(0,"Value","Value of $val1 is "&$val2)
29   │  └─    EndIf
30   ┌─ Else
31   │      MsgBox(0,"Compare","Unable to compare")
32   │
33   │  ┌─    If $val1=15 Then
34   │  ├─        MsgBox(0,"Value","Value of $val1 is "&$val1)
35   │  ┌─    Else
36   │  │         MsgBox(0,"Value","Value of $val1 is not equal to 15")
37   │  ├─    EndIf
38   └─ EndIf
```

Fig 7.8 Nested If statement

In the above example, I added a Nested If...ElseIf statement in the entire If..Else..EndIf statements.

We will discuss the Nested If..ElseIf statement in first If statement.

If $val1=$val2 Then

MsgBox(0,"Compare"," $val1 and $val2 are equal")

If $val=15 Then

MsgBox(0,"Value","Value of $val1 is "&$val1)

ElseIf $val2=16 Then

MsgBox(0,"Value","Value of $val1 is "&$val2)

EndIf

The compiler compares the $val1 and $val2 values, and if it's true then it transfers the control to the instructions present inside the If statement.Otherwise it skips the If statement and starts compiling the ElseIf statement.

When $val1 is equal to $val2 then it will display the message "$val1 and $val2 are equal." After the user clicks the "OK" button, it starts compiling the Nested If statement. When $val1=15 is true then again it displays the message "Value of $val1 is 15." It starts checking the condition of the ElseIf statement, and if none of the conditions in the Nested If statements are true then no action will take place.

You should notice that both of the conditions in the nested if statements are true i.e. $val1=15 are true and $val2=16 are also true.

However, it's not evaluated because in If..else statement when more than one statement becomes true, then the condition which first becomes true will be executed.

In our case, it satisfies the condition $val1<$val2 so it will display the message "$val1 is lesser than $val2" and after the user clicks the Ok button it displays the message "Value of $val1 is15."

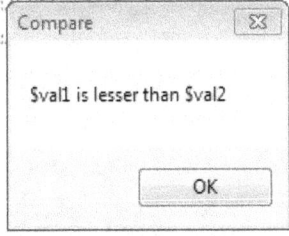

Fig 7.9 Output

Select case statements

AutoIT supports Select Case statements. If you need to check multiple conditions then you can use Select case statement.

In select case statements, cases execute from top to bottom, and if any condition becomes true then the compiler executes the instructions given in that case.

If more than one case statement becomes true then the condition which first becomes true will be executed.

Suppose none of the cases match.Then, instructions in the case else statement will be executed. If no case else statement is present and no cases become true, then the compiler won't perform any action. It comes out of the selected case statement and starts executing the line next to the Select case statement.

Syntax

```
Select

        Case <Condition1>

                <Instructions>..

        Case <Condition2>

                <Instructions>..

        Case <Condition3>

                <Instructions>..

        Case Else

                <Instructions>..

End Select
```

Example 7.6

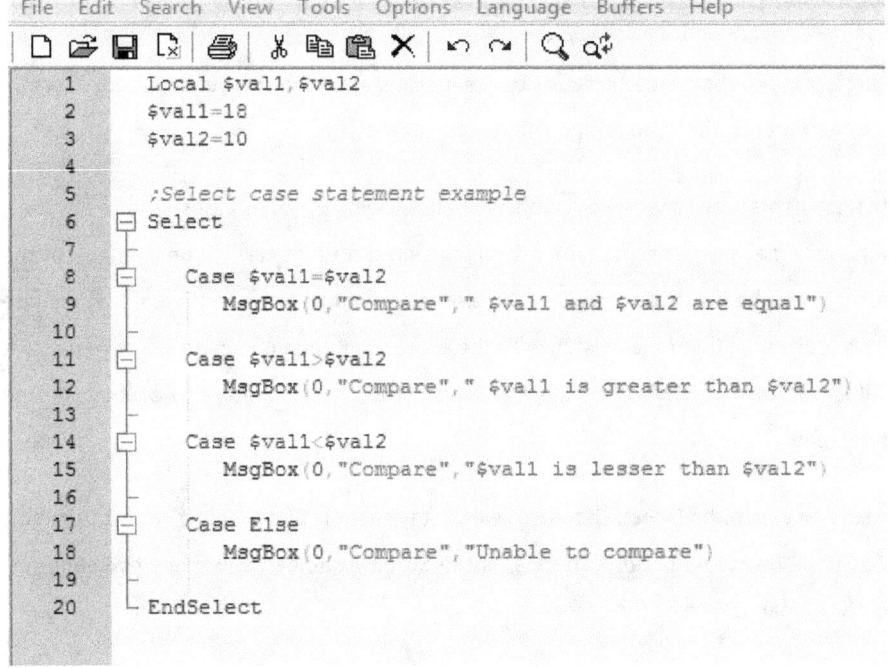

Fig 7.10 Select case statement

I Just replaced our previous If..Else statement with a Select Case statement and changed the values of $val1 & $val2.

The compiler starts compiling the Select case statements starting from top to bottom.

The first case $val1=$val2 checks for the equality of two variables, but it's not equal so it transfers the control to the next case.

The second case $val1>$val2 checks whether 18 is greater than 10 and it's true so it displays the message "$val1 is greater than $val2." After this message box, the compiler comes out of the select case statement.

Select case statements also support nested select case statements.

Switch Statement

Switch statements are the best alternative to the If else statements. If your script consists of a lot of If else statements, then you can go with Switch statements.

In switch statements, the given expression is checked with multiple cases, and if any case matches then the compiler executes the instructions given in that case. Suppose none of the cases match. Then, the instructions in the case else statement will be executed. If no case else statement is present and no cases match with the expression, then no action will take place. It is more effective than multiple If..Else statements. Switch statements also support nested switch statements.

The difference between the Select..Case and Switch statement is that in select case statements, the condition will be evaluated in each case, but in Switch statements, a single condition (or) expression is compared with all the cases.

Syntax

Switch <Expression>

    Case <Value>

        <Instruction>

    Case <Value>

        <Instruction>

    Case <Value>

        <Instruction>

    Case Else

<Instruction>

EndSwitch

Example 7.7

```
File  Edit  Search  View  Tools  Options  Language  Buffers  Help

1       Local $val1,$val2
2       $val1=18
3
4       ;Switch statement example
5       Switch $val1
6
7           Case 1 To 5
8               MsgBox(0,"Compare","The value lies between 1 to 5")
9
10          Case 5 To 15
11              MsgBox(0,"Compare"," The value lies between 5 to 15")
12
13          Case 15 To 20
14              MsgBox(0,"Compare","The value lies between 15 to 20")
15
16          Case Else
17              MsgBox(0,"Compare","Unable to determine the range")
18
19      EndSwitch
```

Fig 7.11 Switch statement

I declared and initialized a variable $val1 to 18. Using a Switch statement, I'm trying to find the range of the variable $val1.

In the first case, it checks whether $val1 lies between 1 and 5 and if it's true then the corresponding message box will be displayed. If not, it transfers the control to the next case.

In the second case, it checks whether $val1 lies between 5 and 15 and if it's true then the corresponding message box will be displayed. If not, it transfers the control to the next case.

The compiler did the same thing as it did for the above two cases. The third case is true, so the message box will be displayed. Suppose none of the cases match. Then, it will display the message "unable to determine the range."

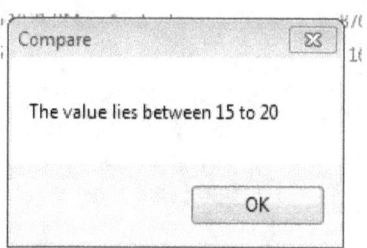

Fig 7.12 Output

8) Iteration statements

AutoIT's iteration statements are for, while, Do..Until. These statements are also called loop statements. This kind of statement continuously iterates and executes the same set of instructions until the condition is met. We will look at each statement in detail.

For..To..Step...Next

This is one of the most commonly used loop statements. It executes and repeats the instructions present inside the loop for a specified number of times. It contains a variable initialized with a value and it acts as a counter for the loop. By default, it increments the value of the counter variable by 1 after every iteration of the For loop. It exits the iteration only if the counter variable meets the stop value. You have an option to increment or decrement the counter variable after iteration by using the Step keyword.

Syntax

For <variable>=<Start value> To <Stop Value> [Step <Step value>]

      <Instructions>

Next

Parameters

Variable- It denotes the variable used of the count

Start value-It denotes the starting value of the counter variable

Stop value-It denotes the final value of the counter variable

Step(Optional)- It is used to increment or decrement the counter variable after iteration

Step value- It denotes the value by which counter is increased or decreased after iteration.

Example 8.1

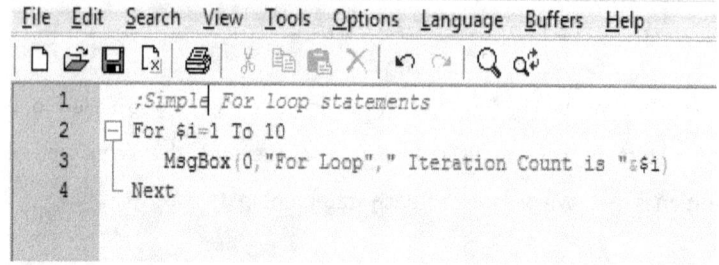

Fig 8.1 Simple For Loop

In example 8.1, the For loop is initialized with variable $i and with start value 1. Each time the message box is displayed, the counter variable $i is increased by 1. So, the message box will be displayed 10 times. The output is shown below:

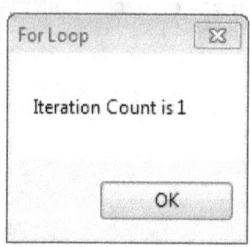

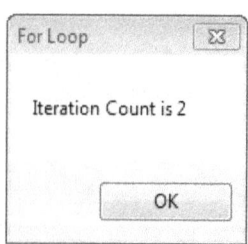

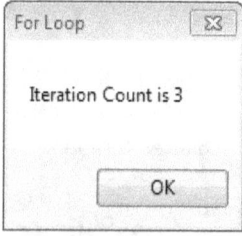

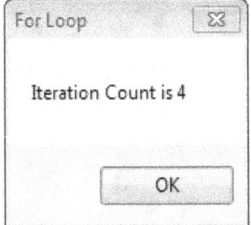

Fig 8.2 Output

The message box will be displayed up to 10 times.

Example 8.2

For loop with step value

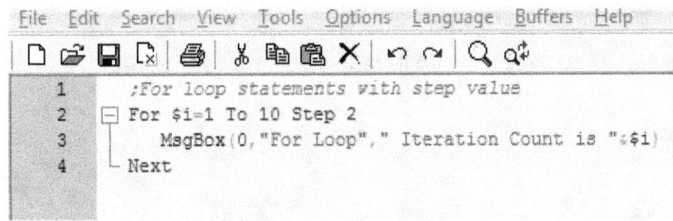

```
1       ;For loop statements with step value
2    ┌  For $i=1 To 10 Step 2
3    │     MsgBox(0,"For Loop"," Iteration Count is "&$i)
4    └  Next
```

Fig 8.3 For Loop statement with Step keyword

I've added the step keyword with value 2 so after each iteration the counter variable $i will be increased by 2 until it reaches the final value 10. The output is shown below:

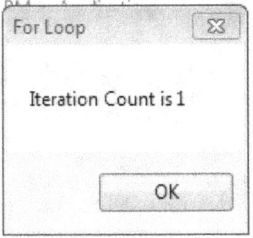

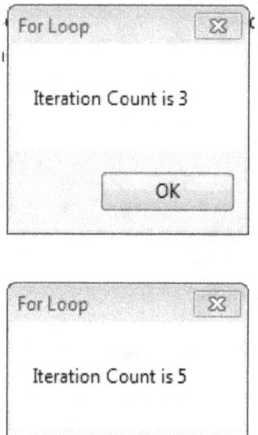

Fig 8.4 Output

The message box will be displayed up to 9 and its stop iteration because the next iteration (11) exceeds the final value (10).

Example 8.3

For loop with decrement counter

```
File  Edit  Search  View  Tools  Options  Language  Buffers  Help

1        ;For loop statements with decrement counter
2      ⊟ For $i=10 To 0 Step -3
3            MsgBox(0,"For Loop"," Iteration Count is ":$i)
4      └ Next
```

Fig 8.5 For loop statement with negative step value

I initialized the variable $i with value 10 and using the step keyword I decrement the counter variable by 3 after each iteration until it reaches the final value. The output is shown below:

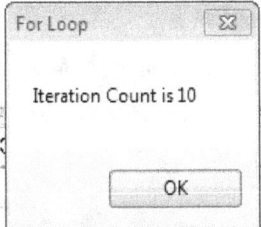

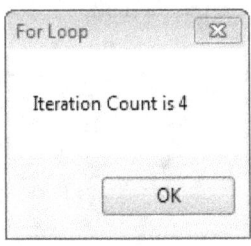

Fig 8.6 Output

For..In..Next

This loop statement iterates through the collection of objects such as array, in a sequential manner from start to finish. The number of iterations of the loop depends upon the number of elements present in the collections. If the object collection doesn't contain any elements then this loop won't be executed. The advantage of this loop statement is that it eliminates the need to use counter variables.

Syntax

For **<Variable>** In **<Collection of objects>**

      <Instructions>

Next

Parameter

Variable- It denotes the local variable which holds an element from collection for iteration. After the end of iteration, the next element in an order will be assigned to this variable.

Collection of objects-It denotes the collection of objects. It should contain at least one element in order to execute this For..In...Next statement.

Example 8.4

In the example below, I declared an array variable called $names to hold up to 6 names and a variable called $combine with an empty string to concatenate the 6 names from the array.

Then, I assigned names to each index of the array variable. With the help of the For..In..Next statement, I can combine all the names and store it in the variable $combine.

$combine=$combine & $ele& " "- This statement combines the names in an array during each iteration.

Initially the value of $combine is "" or empty.

First iteration: In this iteration, the variable $ele holds the value "Tom." So during the iteration, the $combine variable will concatenate the empty or "" value with value "Tom," which results in "Tom."

Second iteration: In this iteration, the variable $ele holds the value "Peter." So during the iteration, the $combine variable will concatenate its previous value with "Peter," which results in "Tom Peter."

Iteration goes on until the last element in an array.

The variable $ele in the loop statement is used to store a single element per iteration starting from index 0 to 5. During every iteration, the $combine variable stores the name of each element by appending it with the previous name as described above. At the last iteration, it is able to combine all the names in the array and store the values within it.

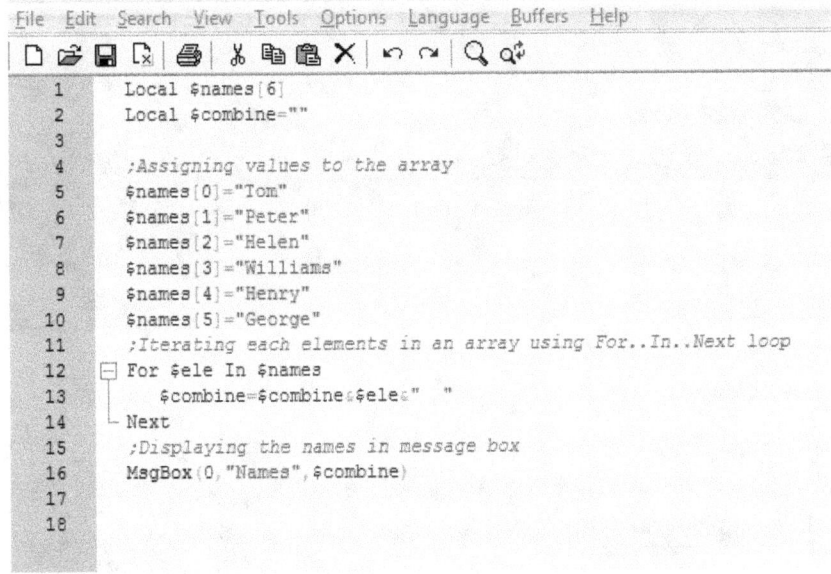

```
     File  Edit  Search  View  Tools  Options  Language  Buffers  Help
    1        Local $names[6]
    2        Local $combine=""
    3
    4        ;Assigning values to the array
    5        $names[0]="Tom"
    6        $names[1]="Peter"
    7        $names[2]="Helen"
    8        $names[3]="Williams"
    9        $names[4]="Henry"
   10        $names[5]="George"
   11        ;Iterating each elements in an array using For..In..Next loop
   12        For $ele In $names
   13            $combine=$combine&$ele&"   "
   14        Next
   15        ;Displaying the names in message box
   16        MsgBox(0, "Names", $combine)
   17
   18
```

Fig 8.7 For..In..Next loop

The output of this script is shown below:

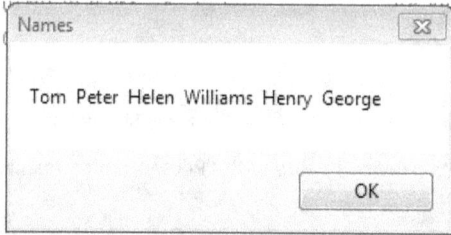

Fig 8.8 Output

Take note of one important point while using this loop statement: the local variable in the For..In...Next statement is "read only" so you cannot alter the content of elements in the collection. In other words, you cannot alter the content of an array using For..In...Next.

To alter the content of array you need to use For..To..Next statement. Let's look at an example.

Example 8.5

```
1        Local $names[6]
2        Local $combine=""
3
4        ;Assigning values to the array
5        $names[0]="Tom"
6        $names[1]="Peter"
7        $names[2]="Helen"
8        $names[3]="Williams"
9        $names[4]="Henry"
10       $names[5]="George"
11
12       ;Altering the value of an arrray using For..Next loop
13       For $i=0 To 5
14           $names[$i]=$names[$i]&" "&$i
15           $combine=$combine&$names[$i]&"   "
16       Next
17
18       ;Displaying the names in message box
19       MsgBox(0,"Names",$combine)
20
21
```

Fig 8.9 For..In..Next loop

I didn't change anything in the declaration and assignment part of variables $names and $combine. I replaced For..In..Next with For..To..Next statement.

In the For statement, I declared the counter variable $i and initialized with start value 0 because the array index always starts with 0. In our example, the array contains 6 names, so I end up with a final value of 5.

I'm trying to alter the names in the array by appending its corresponding index value at the end of each name. In other words, I'm trying to alter the name "Tom" with "Tom 0" and "Peter" with "Peter 1."

$names[$i] = $names[$i]& " " & $i - This statement alters the names in the array by combining the name and its corresponding index value during each iteration. For example, the first iteration results in "Tom 0."

$combine =$combine & $names[$i] & " "- This statement combines the recently altered names in an array during each iteration.

Initially the value of $combine is "" or empty.

First iteration: In this iteration, the variable $names[$i] holds the value "Tom 0," so during iteration, the $combine variable concatenates the empty or "" value with the value "Tom 0" which results in "Tom 0."

Second iteration: In this iteration, the variable $names[$i] holds the value "Peter 1," so during iteration, the $combine variable concatenates its previous value with the value "Peter 1" which results in "Tom 0 Peter 1."

The iteration continues until the For..Next loop reaches its final value, 5.Output of this script is shown below:

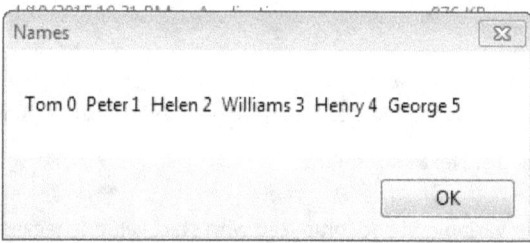

Fig 8.10 Output

Do...Until

This is one of the fundamental loop statements in AutoIT. It iterates the statements or instruction within it until the expression is true. This statement will be executed at least one time since the expression is validated at the end of the loop.

Syntax

Do

      <Instructions>

Until **<Condition>**

Parameter

Instructions- It denotes the set of statements to be executed until the condition is true.

Condition-It specifies the logic to validate during the iteration of the loop. After each iteration, the compiler checks the condition and continues the iteration only when the condition is true.

Example 8.6

In the example below, I declared and initialized two variables($val1 and $i). $val1 is used to store the summation of value during each iteration, and $i acts as a counter variable.

   $val1=$val1+$i- This statement adds the $val1 and $i and stores it in the same variable $val1 during each iteration.

$i=$i+1$-This statement increments the value by 1 after each iteration.

Until($i=10$)- This statement checks that the value of variable i is lesser than or equal to 10 after each iteration. If it exceeds, then the loop stops its iteration.

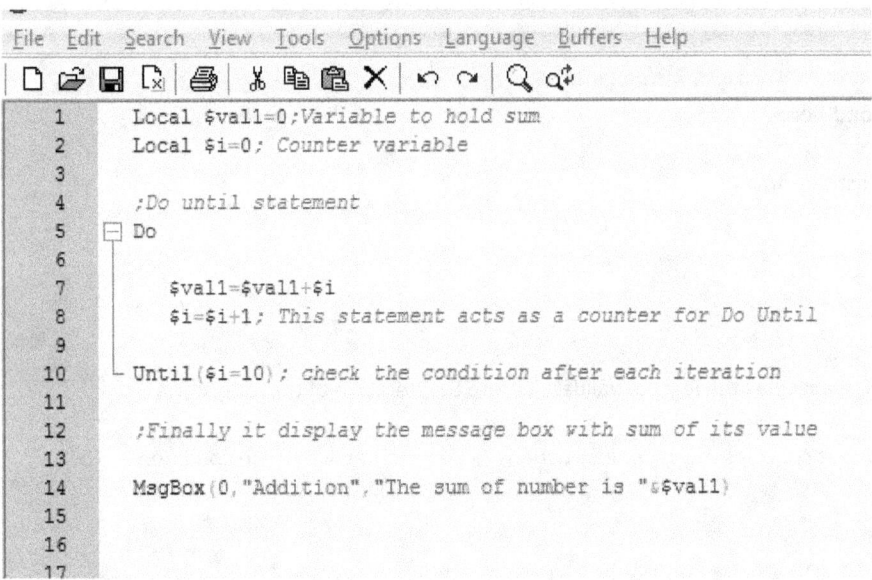

Fig 8.11 Do..Until loop

Finally, it displays the sum of 1 to 10 in the message box.

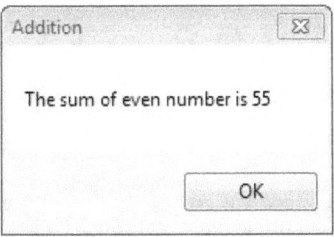

Fig 8.12 Output

While..Wend

It also iterates the statements or instructions within it until the expression is true, like the Do..Until statement. This statement will be executed zero time or more times since the expressions are validated at the beginning of the loop.

Syntax

While **<Condition>**

  <Instructions>

Wend

Parameter

Condition- It specifies the logic to validate before the iteration of the loop starts.

Instructions- It specifies the set of instructions to be executed when the condition is true.

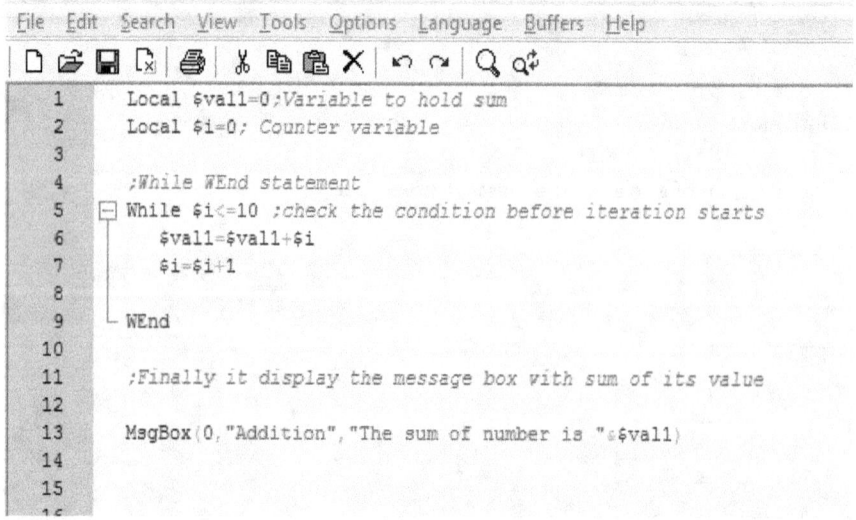

```
1      Local $val1=0 ;Variable to hold sum
2      Local $i=0; Counter variable
3
4      ;While WEnd statement
5    ⊟ While $i<=10 ;check the condition before iteration starts
6          $val1=$val1+$i
7          $i=$i+1
8
9    └ WEnd
10
11     ;Finally it display the message box with sum of its value
12
13     MsgBox(0,"Addition","The sum of number is "&$val1)
14
15
```

Fig 8.13 While..Wend loop

I replaced the Do..Until statement with While..Wend.Take note that I've used **Until $i=10** as a condition in the Do..Until loop, but here I've used **while $i<=10**. The Do..until function iterates the loop until the condition is true, but the While..Wend iterates only if the condition is true. So, when we initialize the counter as **$i=0** and condition as **While $i=10** instead of **While $i<=10** in the While..Wend loop, the compiler compares $i=0 and $i=10. But it fails, so no action will take place. The output is shown below:

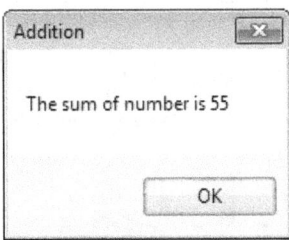

Fig 8.14 Output

AutoIT also allows us to create an infinite loop using the while..Wend statement. To do that, you have to give the condition as any non-zero number. It will execute for an infinite number of times.

Example 8.7

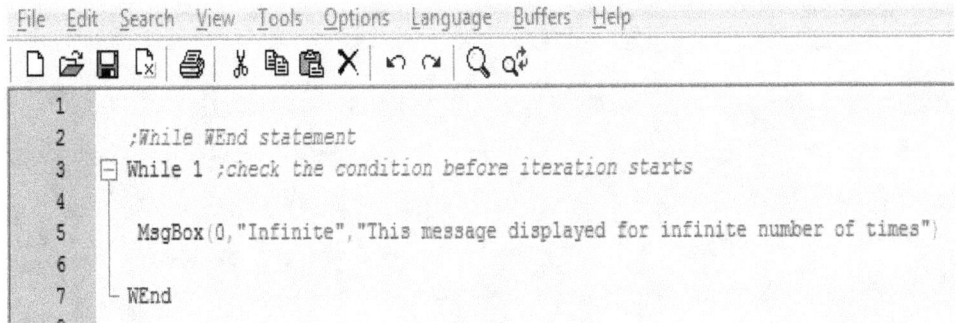

Fig 8.15 Infinite While..Wend loop

In the above example, I initialized an expression with 1 so it will always be true and the While..Wend loop keeps on iterating for an infinite number of times.

9) Jump statements

AutoIT supports Jump statements such as ContinueCase, ContinueLoop, Exit and ExitLoop. The purpose of the Jump statement is to transfer the control to another part of the program. It plays a vital role in the script to avoid run time errors or overflow.

ContinueCase

This statement can be used only within the Select..case and Switch statement. You cannot use the ContinuCase elsewhere. Otherwise, it will cause a fatal error.

To be more specific, this statement can only be used within the cases of Select and Switch statements. When the compiler finds this statement in any case, it stops executing the remaining set of statements present after the ContinueCase and starts executing the next case without verifying its condition.

It won't verify whether the next case met the specified condition or not, and will simply execute the code within the next case. Be aware that to execute the next case statement using continuecase, the case that the continuecase statement belongs to should meet the condition of the Select or Switch statement.

ContinueCase in Select statement

Syntax

Select

    Case <Condition1>

        <Instructions>..

    ContinueCase

    Case <Condition2>

<Instructions>..

Case <Condition3>

<Instructions>..

Case Else

<Instructions>..

End Select

Example 9.1

```
     File  Edit  Search  View  Tools  Options  Language  Buffers  Help

1        Local $val1,$val2
2        $val1=20
3        $val2=20
4
5        ;Select case statement with continucase
6      ⊟ Select
7      ├
8      ⊟   Case $val1=$val2
9      │      MsgBox(0,"Compare","Value 1 and Value 2 are equal")
10     │      ContinueCase
11     ├      MsgBox(0,"Verify","This message box won't populate")
12     ⊟   Case $val1>$val2
13     ├      MsgBox(0,"Verify","This case statement condition is not validated by the compiler")
14     ⊟   Case $val1<$val2
15     ├      MsgBox(0,"Compare","Value 1 is lesser than value 2")
16     ⊟   case Else
17     │      MsgBox(0,"Compare","Unable to compare")
18     │
19     └ EndSelect
20
```

Fig 9.1 Continuecase in select case statement

I declared and initialized two variables($val1 and $val2) with value 20. With the help of the select case statement, I'm checking multiple cases for those two variables.

In the first case, I'm checking for equality.It satisfies the condition, so the compiler starts executing the statement within the first case.

First it displays a message box "Value 1 and Value 2 are equal." After the user clicks the OK button, the compiler begins compiling the ContinueCase statement. As soon as the compiler detects this statement,it stops executing any further statements in the first case and starts executing the statements in the next case without validating its condition.

The second case checks whether Value 1 is greater than value 2.It fails, but the compiler still displays the message box "This case statement condition is not validated by the compiler" inside the Second case and comes out of the Select..Case statement. The output of the program is shown below:

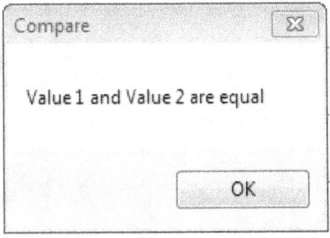

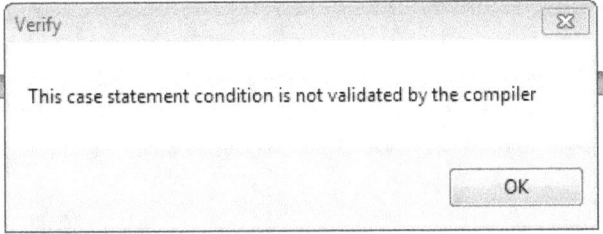

Fig 9.2 Output

ContinueCase in Switch Statement

Syntax

Switch <Expression>

    Case <Value>

        <Instructions>

        <ContinueCase>...

        <Instructions>

    Case <Value>

        <Instructions>

    Case <Value>

        <Instructions>

    Case Else

        <Instructions>

EndSwitch

It behaves the same way in both the switch statement and the select case statement.

Example 9.2

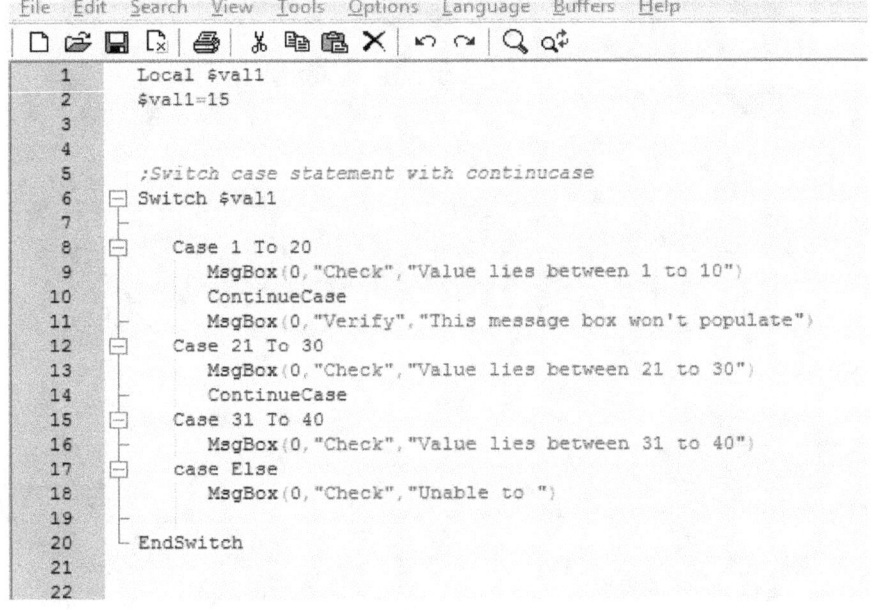

```
1        Local $val1
2        $val1=15
3
4
5        ;Switch case statement with continucase
6    ⊟   Switch $val1
7    ├
8    ⊟       Case 1 To 20
9                MsgBox(0,"Check","Value lies between 1 to 10")
10               ContinueCase
11   ├           MsgBox(0,"Verify","This message box won't populate")
12   ⊟       Case 21 To 30
13               MsgBox(0,"Check","Value lies between 21 to 30")
14   ├           ContinueCase
15   ⊟       Case 31 To 40
16   ├           MsgBox(0,"Check","Value lies between 31 to 40")
17   ⊟       case Else
18               MsgBox(0,"Check","Unable to ")
19   ├
20   └   EndSwitch
21
22
```

Fig 9.3 Continuecase in switch statement

Notice that in example 9.2, I've used two ContinueCase statements in two different cases. This switch statement evaluates the value of variable $val1 in all the cases.

The condition of the switch statement is satisfied in the first case, so it displays the message "Value lies between 1 to 10," but since the ContinueCase statement is present, it skips the case and starts executing the statements in the second case without evaluating its condition. It displays the message "Value lies between 21 to 30" even though it doesn't belong to that range.In the second case, the compiler again finds the ContinueCase statement, so it starts executing the instructions in the third case without evaluating its condition. It displays another message box saying "Value lies between 31 to 40." The output of program is shown below:

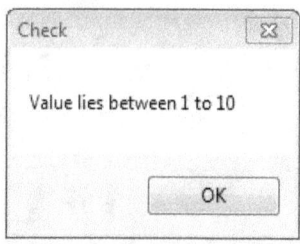

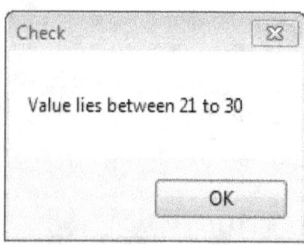

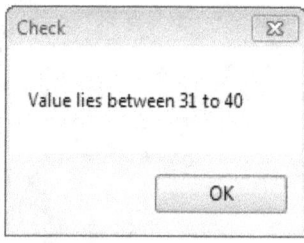

Fig 9.4 Output

Continue Loop

The ContinueLoop statement should be useful when you want to continue running the loop, but it should not execute statements present in the loop after the ContinueLoop statement. In some cases, we need to jump to the next iteration of the loop when it meets the specified condition.You can achieve this with the ContinueLoop statement. You can use this statement in Do..Until, While..Wend and For loop.

Syntax

ContinueLoop [Level]

Parameter

Level (Optional)- It denotes the level of loop to restart. By default the value is 1. If the Level is negative or zero then no action will be taken.

ContinueLoop in Do..Until Loop

Syntax

Do

       <Instructions>

       If <Condition> Then

              ContinueLoop

       EndIf

       <Instructions>

Until **<Condition>**

Example 9.3

```
1     Local $val1=0;Counter variable
2     Local $combine="" ;variable used to combine numbers
3
4  Do
5
6         $val1=$val1+1
7         ;It skip the Do loop when $val1 is 4 or $val1 is 7
8
9         If $val1=4 or $val1=7 Then
10            ContinueLoop
11        EndIf
12
13        $combine=$combine&" "&$val1
14
15   Until ($val1=10)
16
17   MsgBox (0,"Values","The values are " &$combine)
18
19
```

Fig 9.5 ContinueLoop in Do..Until statement

Two variables are declared in which $val1 acts as a counter variable and $combine is used to concatenate the numbers. I've used the continueLoop statement to continue the loop without concatenating the value to the variable $combine when the value of $val1 is either 4 or 7.For all other cases, it combines the numbers and stores it in the variable $combine. The Do until loop iterates until the variable $val1 becomes 10. Finally, the message box displays all of the numbers from 1 to 10 except 4 and 7.

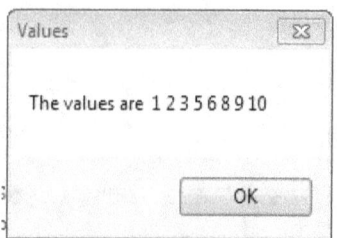

Fig 9.6 Output

The ContinueLoop statement behaves in the same way as the While..Wend loop.

ContinueLoop in For..Next Loop

ContinueLoop can also be used in the For..Next Loop. If continueLoop is present anywhere inside the For..Next Loop, then the compiler starts executing the next iteration of the loop after it reaches the ContinueLoop statement. It is also possible to iterate the next loop when the specified condition is satisfied, like the Do..While Loop.

Syntax

```
For <variable>=<Start value> To <Stop Value> [Step <Step value>]

        <Instructions>

        If <Condition> Then

                ContinueLoop

        EndIf

        <Instructions>

Next
```

Example 9.4

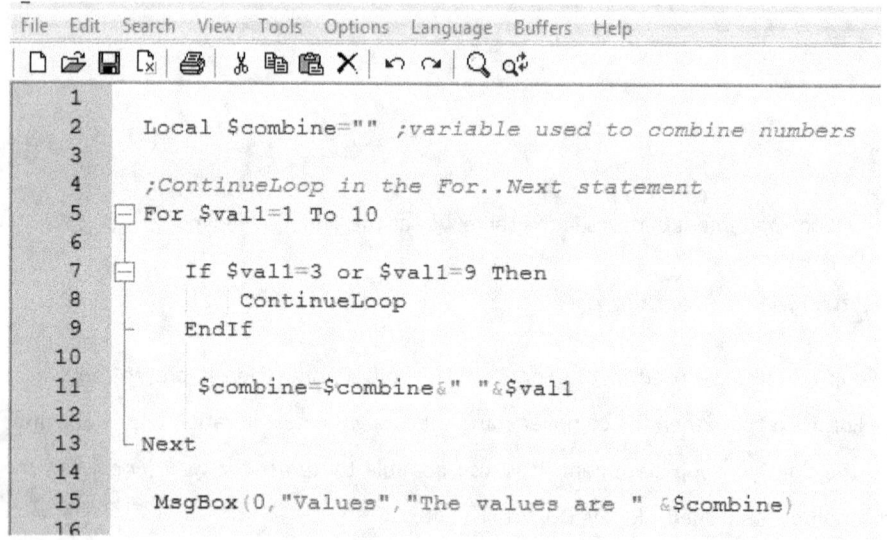

Fig 9.7 Continue Loop in For...Next loop

I Just replaced the Do..Until statement in example 9.3 with the For...Next Loop. It starts iterating from $val1 to 10 and skips its iteration when $val1 is 3 or 9. During each iteration, the value of the variable $val1 is concatenated in the $combine variable. The final output is shown below:

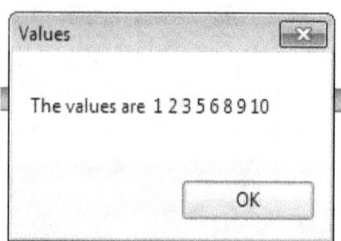

Fig 9.8 Output

The ContinueLoop statement behaves in the same way as the For..In..Next loop.

ContineLoop with Level

From the syntax of ContinueLoop, you might be aware that it accepts a parameter called Level. This level should be a non-negative numerical value. If the continue loop statement lies within the multiple loops, then this level denotes from where it should restart the iteration. By default, the current loop will be restarted. If you specify the value as 2 and multiple loops are present, then it restarts the iteration starting from one loop outer than the current loop. You can use the ContinueLoop statement inside the For , Do..Until & While..Wend loop.

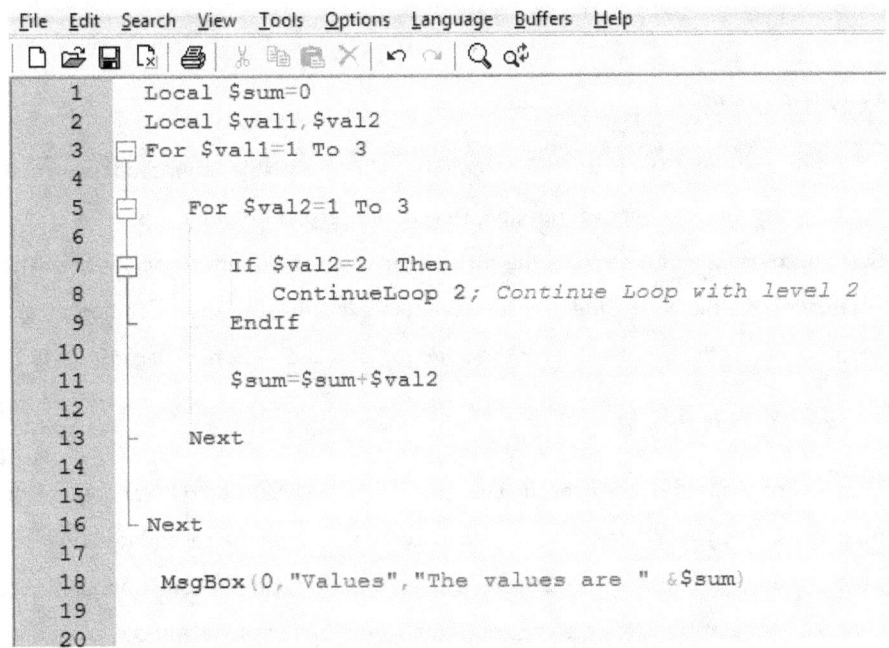

```
File  Edit  Search  View  Tools  Options  Language  Buffers  Help

 1       Local $sum=0
 2       Local $val1, $val2
 3     ⊟ For $val1=1 To 3
 4
 5     ⊟    For $val2=1 To 3
 6
 7     ⊟       If $val2=2   Then
 8                ContinueLoop 2;  Continue Loop with level 2
 9             EndIf
10
11             $sum=$sum+$val2
12
13          Next
14
15
16    └ Next
17
18       MsgBox (0, "Values", "The values are  " &$sum)
19
20
```

Fig 9.9 Continue loop with level

The logic behind the loop will **be a bit complicated** unless you understand how the nested for loop works.

Suppose the outer for loop iterates from 1 to x and the inner for loop iterates from 1 to y. Then during the first iteration of the outer for loop, when the outer for loop variable is 1 then it executes the inner for loop by iterating it's variable from 1 to y.

After the inner for loop finishes the iteration up to its final value, the outer for loop starts the second iteration. Also, during the second iteration of the outer for loop, when the outer for loop variable is 2 then it executes the inner for loop by iterating its variable from 1 to y. Then the cycle repeats until the outer for loop reaches its final value.

Let's look at our example. I've used the statement ContinueLoop 2, which starts the next iteration of the Outer for loop when the inner for loop variable is 2. Let's look into the concept behind it.

Outer For loop -First iteration

The inner For loop completes the first iteration and the value of variable $sum changes from 0 to 1. Then, it should start the second iteration. During the second iteration the value of the variable $val2 becomes 2 and it satisfies the If condition. So, the ContinueLoop 2 statement transfers the control to the Next Outer For loop without executing the third iteration of the inner for loop. So, during the first iteration of the outer for loop, the value of variable $sum is 1.

Outer For loop- second iteration

Again, the inner for loop completes the first iteration and the value of the variable $sum changes from 1 to 2. Then, it should start the second iteration. During the second iteration the value of the variable $val2 becomes 2 and it again satisfies the If condition. So, the ContinueLoop 2 statement transfers the control to the Next Outer for loop without executing the third iteration of the inner for loop. So, during the second iteration of the outer for loop, the value of the variable $sum is 2.

Outer For loop- third iteration

Again, the inner for loop completes the first iteration and the value of the variable $sum changes from 2 to 3. Then, it should start the second iteration. During the second iteration the value of the variable $val2 becomes 2 and it again satisfies the If condition. So, the ContinueLoop 2 stops iterating the outer for loop since it reach its final value. So, during the third iteration of the outer for loop, the value of the variable $sum is 3 .

The output is shown below:

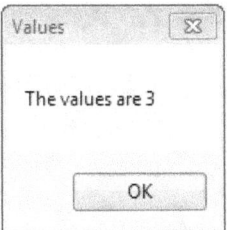

Fig 9.10 Output

ExitLoop

The function of the ExitLoop statement is to terminate the loop and to stop its iteration. It will be useful for testing the functionality of the loop body. You can also use it when an error occurs or when an exception happens during run time. The ExitLoop statement can be used in the While..Wend Loop, Do...While Loop and For loop. You can use the ExitLoop statement inside the For, Do..Until& While..Wend loop.

The ContinueLoop continues the next iteration of the loop, but Exitloop terminates and its execution.

Syntax

ExitLoop [level]

Parameter

Level (Optional)- It denotes the level of loop to exit. By default the value is 1. If the Level is negative or zero then no action will be taken.

ExitLoop in Do..Until

Syntax

Do

        <Instructions>

        If <Condition> Then

                ExitLoop

        EndIf

        <Instructions>

Until **<Condition>**

Example 9.5

```
File  Edit  Search  View  Tools  Options  Language  Buffers  Help

 1        Local $val=0;Counter variable
 2
 3    ┌ Do
 4
 5            $val=$val+1
 6
 7    ┌       If $val=6 Then
 8                ExitLoop
 9    └       EndIf
10
11    └ Until($val=10)
12
13        MsgBox(0,"Iteration", "Loop exit when the iteration count is "&$val)
14
```

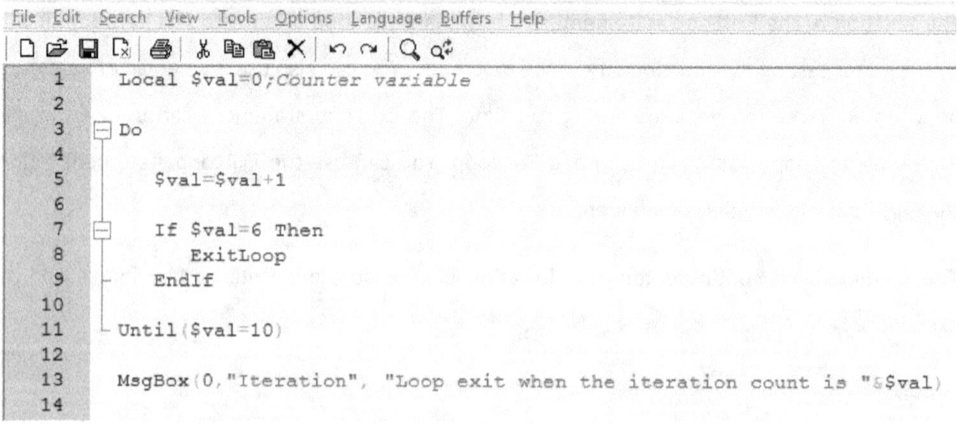

Fig 9.11 ExitLoop in Do..Until loop

Using the Do..Until loop, I start iterating from 1 to 10 with the help of the counter variable $val. I've used the Exit loop statement to exit the Do..Until loop when the value variable becomes 6. So, after each iteration the compiler checks the value of the variable with the condition given in the If statement. Using the message box, I've displayed the iteration count when it exits the Do..Until Loop. The output is shown below:

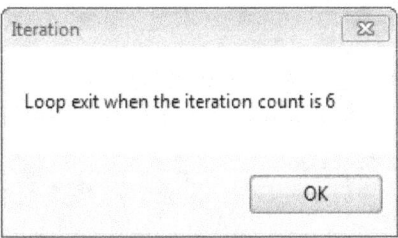

Fig 9.12 Output

ExitLoop in For..Next Loop

This can also be used in the For..Next loop to terminate its iteration. If ExitLoop is present anywhere inside the For..Next Loop, then the compiler terminates further execution and transfers the control to the statement present next to the For..Next loop.

Syntax

For <variable>=<Start value> To <Stop Value> [Step <Step value>]

    <Instructions>

    If <Condition> Then

        ExitLoop

    EndIf

    <Instructions>

Next

Example 9.6

```
File  Edit  Search  View  Tools  Options  Language  Buffers  Help

 1
 2
 3    ⊟ For $val=1 to 10
 4
 5    ⊟     If $val=6 Then
 6              ExitLoop
 7      └     EndIf
 8
 9    └ Next
10
11      MsgBox(0,"Iteration", "Loop exit when the iteration count is "&$val)
12
```

Fig 9.13 ExitLoop in For..Next statement

I replaced the Do..Until loop in example 9.5 with the For..Next loop. The For loop iterates from 1 to 5 and during the 6th iteration, the condition in the If statement becomes true. So, it exits the For loop and starts compiling the statement present next to the For loop. Here, the message box displays the iteration count when it exits the For loop. The output is shown below:

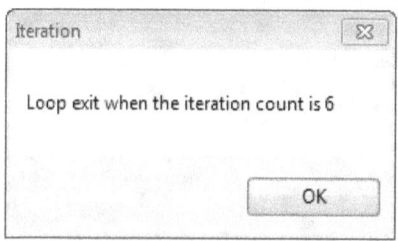

Fig 9.14 Output

ExitLoop with Level

The Exit loop also accepts a parameter called level, much like the Continue Loop. The value of the Level should also be a non-negative numerical value. If it is zero or a negative, then no action will be taken. It indicates the loop level to Exit. Suppose the Exit Loop statement lies inside the multiple loop statement. Then, its level indicates the number of loops to exit starting from the current loop. If the level is not specified, then it exits only from the current loop.

Example 9.7

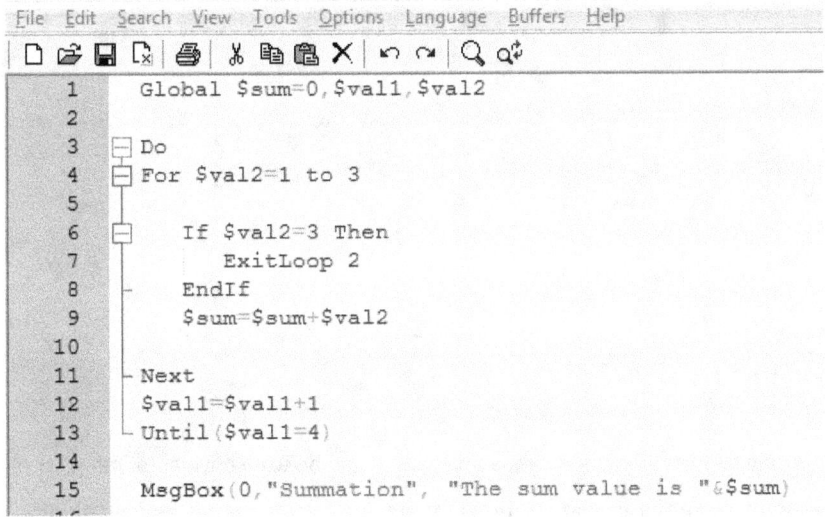

Fig 9.15 ExitLoop with level

I've used two loop statements, For and Do..Until. Working logic of multiple loop statement is the same as the nested For loop statements I demonstrated in the ContineLoop with Level. Let's see how it works.

The Do..Until loop starts its first iteration by default without verifying its condition. Inside the Do..Until loop, the For loop statement exists. The For loop statement starts its first iteration by checking the If condition, and at the end of first iteration the value of variable $sum is 1. Then it starts its second iteration by checking the If condition, and at the end of the second iteration the value of variable $sum is 3 (or the sum of the previous value 1 and current value 2). But during the third iteration, it met the If's condition, so the ExitLoop 2statement should execute. This ExitLoop statement contains a level as 2, so it should exit two levels: loop one being the current For..Next loop(first) and the other being the outer Do..until loop(Second). Then, the compiler compiles the message box statement. The final value of $sum is 3 and will be displayed.

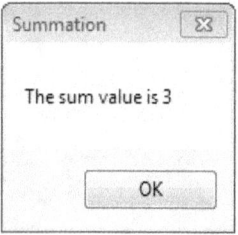

Fig 9.16 Output

Exit

This statement terminates the execution of the program. It can be used anywhere in the script. This statement should be useful to end the program when a fatal error has happened during run time.

Syntax

Exit [Return code]

Parameter

Return code (optional)- It specifies the script return code. By default the value is 0.

You can represent the Exit statement in multiple ways such as Exit, Exit 0, or Exit(0).

Example 9.8

I'm reusing example 9.7 by replacing ExitLoop 2 with Exit 0. So, when the If's condition is met during the iteration of the For loop, the Exit 0 statement terminates the program.

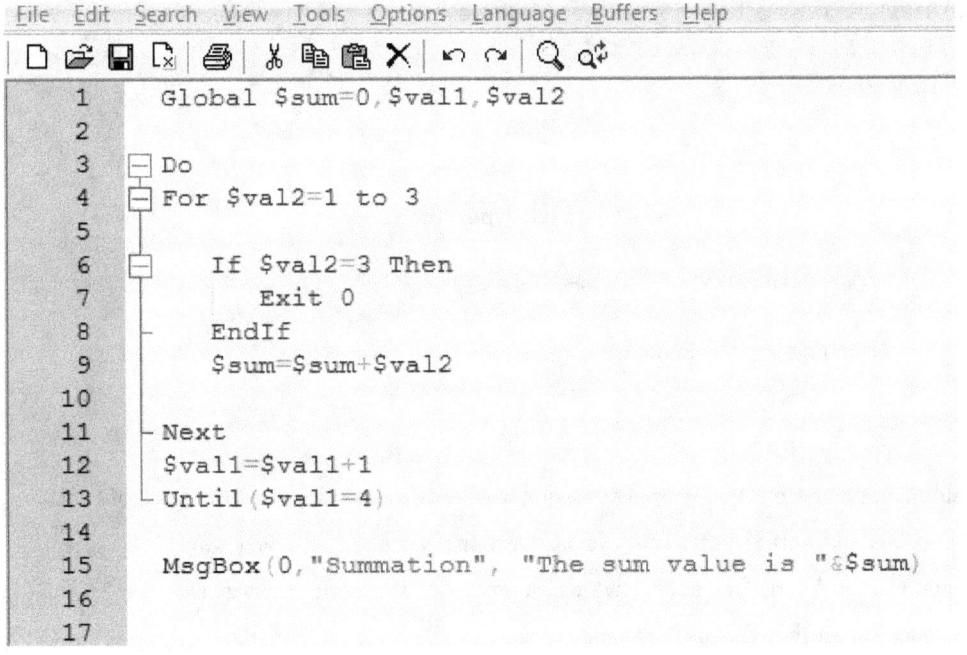

```
File  Edit  Search  View  Tools  Options  Language  Buffers  Help
   1        Global $sum=0,$val1,$val2
   2
   3    ⊟ Do
   4    ⊟ For $val2=1 to 3
   5
   6    ⊟    If $val2=3 Then
   7            Exit 0
   8    ⊢     EndIf
   9          $sum=$sum+$val2
  10
  11    ⊢ Next
  12      $val1=$val1+1
  13    ⊢ Until($val1=4)
  14
  15      MsgBox(0,"Summation", "The sum value is "&$sum)
  16
  17
```

Fig 9.17 Exit statement

10) Declaring and calling Functions

A Function is a set of code that performs a specific task by getting the data, processing it and returning a result. Once a function is written, it can be called to anywhere from anywhere in the script for any number of times. Advantages of functions are:

1) It breaks down the code to sub code for easy understanding and debugging

2) Reusing of code instead of repetitively writing or copying the same code

3) It can be called whenever required

4) Easy to maintain the script

In AutoIT, functions are sub divided into two types. They are:

     1) Built in Functions

     2) User defined Functions

1) Built in functions

AutoIT has numerous built-in functions.in other words, we can say AutoIT is made of Functions. Functions can accept parameters to perform specific tasks in which some parameters are optional. Some functions don't have parameters, but still perform tasks. Examples of Built in functions are msgbox, winactivate and stringlen.

Msgbox function

This is one of the most frequently used built in functions in AutoIT. It displays a message box with a specified message and with specified buttons.

Syntax

Msgbox(Flag, "Title", "Text", [timeout, [hwnd]])

Parameters

Flag- It indicates the type of message box and button combinations. You can use multiple possible combinations of icon and buttons.

Title- It indicates the title of the message box.

Text- It indicates the message to be displayed in the message box.

Timeout (Optional)- It indicates time duration for which the message box should be displayed. By default it stays permanently until it receives a response from the user.

Hwnd(Optional) - It specifies the window handle to use as a parent for this message box.

In the syntax, optional parameters are specified within the square bracket. If you wish to use the optional parameter, then you need to ensure that you have supplied data to all the parameters (including optional) that exist before the specified parameter.

For specified buttons and icons you can use the below table for reference. You can either use a constant name, a decimal flag or a hexadecimal flag in the flag parameter.

You can combine button and Icon, but you cannot combine button with button and icon with icon.

Constant Name	Decimal flag	Button-related result	Hexadecimal flag
$MB_OK	0	OK button	0x0
$MB_OKCANCEL	1	OK and Cancel	0x1
$MB_ABORTRETRYIGNORE	2	Abort, Retry, and Ignore	0x2
$MB_YESNOCANCEL	3	Yes, No, and Cancel	0x3
$MB_YESNO	4	Yes and No	0x4
$MB_RETRYCANCEL	5	Retry and Cancel	0x5
$MB_CANCELTRYCONTINU	6	Cancel, Try Again, Continue	0x6
$MB_HELP	16384	Adds a Help button to the message box	0x4000
Constant Name	decimal flag	Icon-related Result	hexadecimal flag
	0	(No icon)	0x0
$MB_ICONERROR	16	Stop-sign icon	0x10
$MB_ICONQUESTION	32	Question-mark icon	0x20
$MB_ICONWARNING	48	Exclamation-point icon	0x30
$MB_ICONINFORMATION	64	Information-sign icon consisting of an 'i	0x40

Table 10.1 Msgbox constants table

Example 10.1

```
1
2    #include<msgboxconstants.au3>
3    MsgBox($MB_OK&$MB_ICONERROR,"My Title","My message is critical")
4
```

Fig 10.1 Msgbox function

I used a constant name for $MB_OK for the OK button and $MB_ICONERROR for the Error icon.

So, we included msgboxconstants.au3.

Output is shown below:

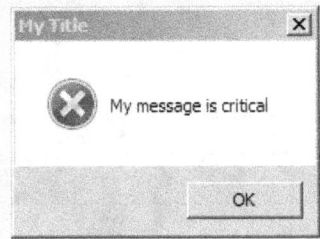

Fig 10.2 Output

Example10. 2

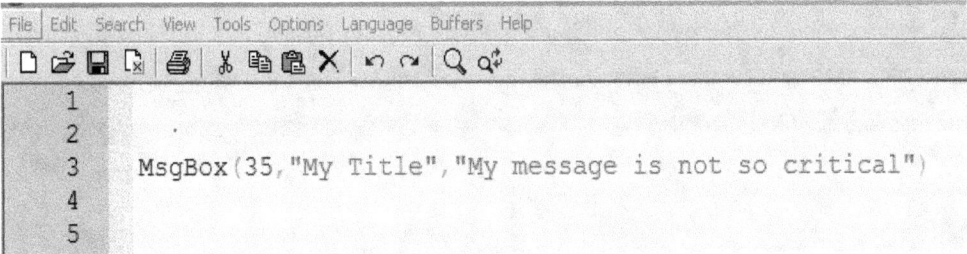

Fig 10.3 Msgbox function

Here I used a decimal value 35 which is the sum of 32 and 3. From the table you can find the type of icon for the decimal value 32 and the type of button for the decimal value 3.

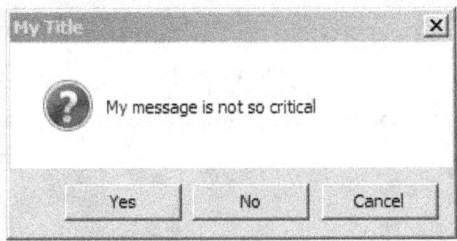

Fig 10.4 Output

Example 10.3

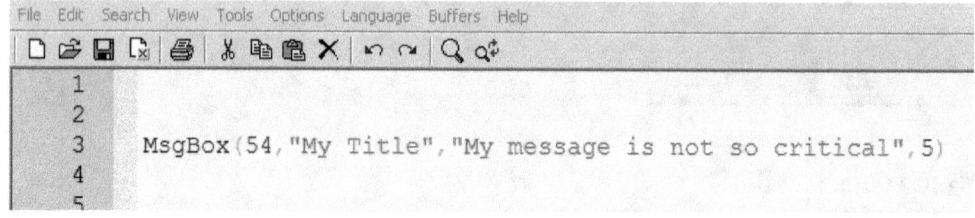

Fig 10.5 Msgbox function

The decimal value 54 is the sum of 48 and 6. 48 displays an Exclamation icon and 6 includes cancel, Try again and continue buttons. The fourth parameter (Timeout) value is 5, so it displays the message box for 5 seconds.

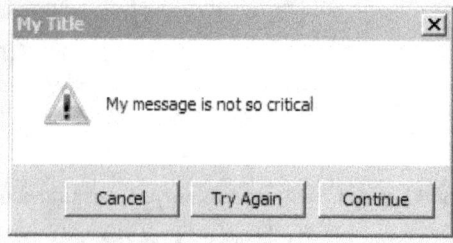

Fig 10.6 Output

As of now we discussed how to use the msgbox function, but one more thing we need to do is act according to a response from the user. To get a response, we can use statements such as If..Else, switch case etc.

To get the response, we need to know the return value of the button given in the table 10.2

Button Pressed	Return Value
OK	$IDOK (1)
CANCEL	$IDCANCEL (2)
ABORT	$IDABORT (3)
RETRY	$IDRETRY (4)
IGNORE	$IDIGNORE (5)
YES	$IDYES (6)
NO	$IDNO (7)
TRY AGAIN **	$IDTRYAGAIN (10)
CONTINUE **	$IDCONTINUE (11)

Table 10.2 Msgbox return button and its value

Example 10.4

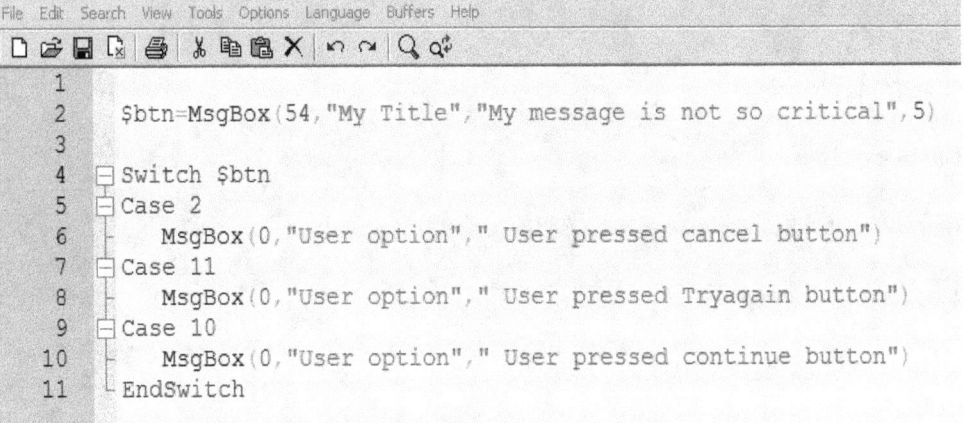

```
1
2    $btn=MsgBox(54,"My Title","My message is not so critical",5)
3
4    Switch $btn
5    Case 2
6       MsgBox(0,"User option"," User pressed cancel button")
7    Case 11
8       MsgBox(0,"User option"," User pressed Tryagain button")
9    Case 10
10      MsgBox(0,"User option"," User pressed continue button")
11   EndSwitch
```

Fig 10.7 Finding msgbox button pressed

In example 10.4, I get to know the button pressed by the user with the help of a switch statement. If the cancel button was pressed, then it returns the value 2(from table 10.2).So, it will execute the script belonging to case 2. Here it displays another message box indicating the button pressed by the user.

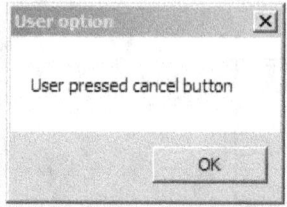

Fig 10.9 Output

Sleep function

This function is used to pause the script for a given time during execution. It is helpful when working with windows. Sometimes we need to pause the script for a few seconds to launch an application, a processing application, or to move from one handle to another handle, etc.

Syntax

Sleep (Time delay)

Parameters

Time delay- It indicates the time to pause the script(millisecond).

1 second= 1000 milliseconds

2)User Defined Functions

Many User defined functions are written by AutoIT users to enhance the functionality of the program. It allows user to create their own user-defined functions. Let's see how to create a user-defined function. It can be defined with or without parameters. When a function is defined without parameters, then it simply executes the script within it on calling the function. When a function is defined with parameters, then while calling it you must pass either a value or a variable as an argument (unless it's an optional parameter). For optional parameters, you may or may not pass a value or a variable. If you don't pass any value or variable to optional parameters, then it takes a default value while defining the function and executes the script.

Syntax

FuncFunctioname([**Const**] [**ByRef**] $param1, ..., [**Const**] [**ByRef**] $paramN, $optionalpar1 = value,$Optinalpar2...)

  [**Return** [*value*]]

EndFunc

Keywords

FuncEndFunc- All user defined functions must start with keyword "Func" and end with keyword "EndFunc"

Const (Optional)- It indicates that the value of the parameter won't be changed during the execution of the function. But you can use the keyword const only if the passing variable must be initialized with the keyword const.

ByRef(Optional)- It creates a link between the new and original variables. So, if this variable is altered within the function, then the value of the original variable is also altered. By default, a copy of the variable is created so it won't make any change to the original variable even if it's altered within the function. You shouldn't alter the content of a variable by declaring a parameter with const and ByRef keyword,or else it will show an error message.

$param1 – It is declared without initializing with a value, which emphasize that this parameter is mandatory. So, when calling this function, you should pass a value or a variable to this parameter.

$optionalpar1 = value- It was declared and initialized with a value, which emphasize that it's an optional parameter. There are certain rules you need to follow while declaring optional parameter(s).

  a) Optional parameters should always be defined as a last parameter.

b) If you are declaring more than one optional parameter, then all the parameter should be listed at the end. You should not shuffle mandatory and optional parameters.

c) Parameters defined after the optional parameter should always be an optional parameter.

Return- It is used to exit the function. It also returns the result of a function to the function call after executing the function.

Example 10.5

```
File Edit Search View Tools Options Language Buffers Help

1    ;Declaring variable
2
3    $val1=10
4    Const $val2=35
5    $val3=5
6
7    ;Calling function in MsgBox
8    MsgBox(0,"My function"," Value returned by myfunction is "& myfunction($val1,$val2,$val3))
9
10   ;Defining the function
11   Func myfunction(ByRef $num1, Const $num2, $num3, $num4=20, $num5=30)
12       $ret=$num1+$num2+$num3+$num4+$num5
13       Return $ret
14   EndFunc
15
```

Fig 10.10 Defining function

I defined a function, called myfucntion, which can hold up to 5 parameters out of which 2 parameters are optional.

Parameters to be passed to the functions are declared initially. I passed three variable $val1, $val2 and $val3 as parameters to myfunction in the msgbox function.

The statement myfunction($val1,$val2,$val3) contains only three parameters and will take the default value for the 4th and 5th parameter while calling and compiling the script within it.(I.e. add all the variables and finally return the output variable $ret to the function call).

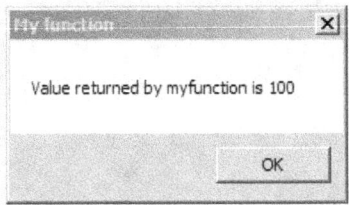

Fig 10.11 Output

Example 10.6

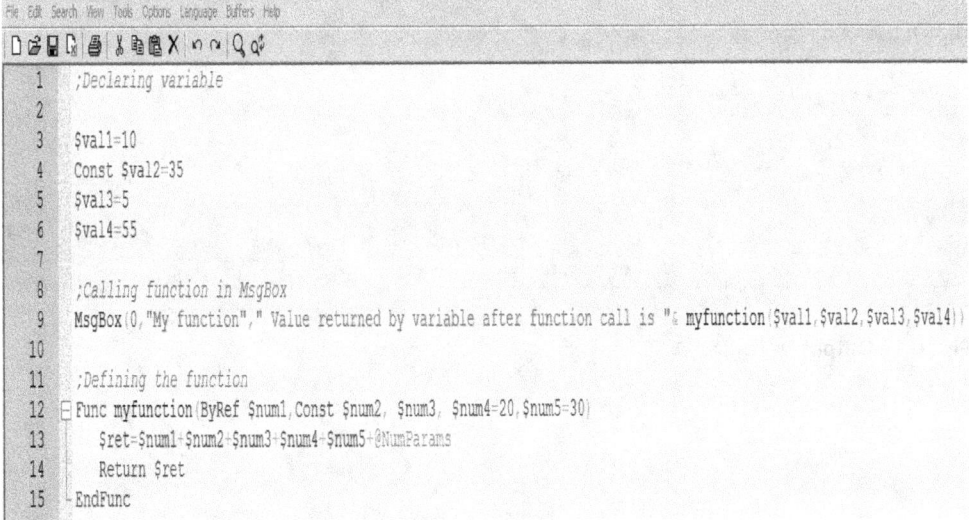

Fig 10.11 Defining function with optional parameters

I'm calling myfunction with four parameters. The fourth parameter is optional, so when we pass any value it will take up the value or it will take the default value while declaring the function. Here in the fourth parameter I've passed variable $val4 which contains value 55, so it will pass it as an argument.

I've also used a macro, @NumParams, which is used to determine the number of parameters given while calling function. Here it returns the value 4 since our myfunction contains four parameters. The function will add all variable as well as @NumParams and store it in $ret and return to the msgbox.

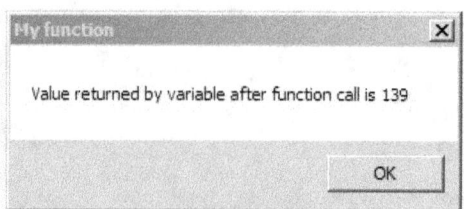

Fig 10.12 Output

11) String Functions

A String is a collection of characters containing numerals, alphabetical characters and special characters. Sometimes, we may need to manipulate, sort, convert, compare, format or edit the input string for manipulation. By default,AutoIT comes with numerous functions for string handling. Let's look at the most useful string functions in detail.

StringLower

This function converts the given input string to lowercase letters. If a string contain upper case, then it converts it into lower case (for lower cases and special characters no conversion will take place).

Syntax

StringLower("String")

Parameters

String- It denotes the string which you need to convert into lowercase letters

Example 11.1

```
File Edit Search View Tools Options Language Buffers Help

1    ;Declare and initializing variables
2    Local $mystring="### Hello World ! This is my First String #####"
3
4    ;convert it to lower case using string function
5    $convt=StringLower($mystring)
6
7    ;Displaying it
8    MsgBox(0,"Convert"," String after converision become "&$convt)
9
10
```

Fig 11.1 StringLower function

I declared a variable $mystring and assigned a string "### Hello World ! This is my First String #####" to it. Take note that it contains a combination of lowercase letters, uppercase letters and special characters. In the second statement, I pass this string as an argument to function StringLower and assign it to a variable $convt.

Msgbox finally displays the string after converting its uppercase letters to lowercase letters. But this function won't alter the lowercase letters, symbols and special characters.

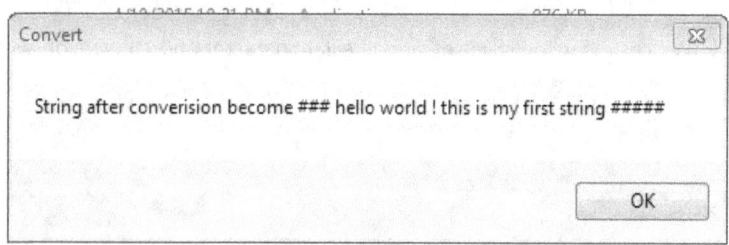

Fig 11.2 Output

StringIsLower

This function returns true if the string contains only lower case letter(s) and in all other cases like whitespaces, digits and special characters it return false.

Syntax

StringIsLower("String")

Parameters

String-It denotes the string to evaluate

Example 11.2

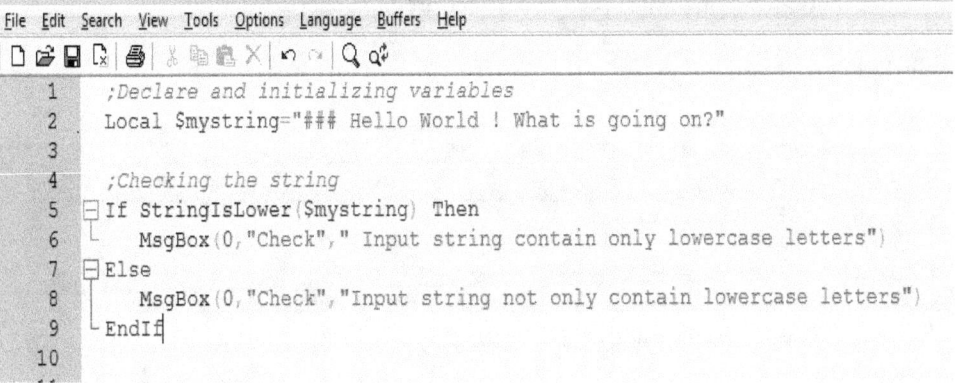

Fig 11.3 StringIsLowerfucntion

The variable $mystring contains a combination of lowercase, uppercase, symbols and white space. So this function returns false upon evaluation. Output is shown below:

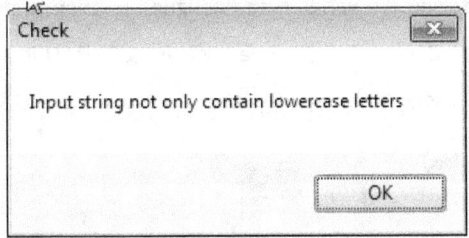

Fig 11.4 Output

String Upper

This function converts the given input string to uppercase letters. If a string contains lowercase letters then it converts it into uppercase, butwon't alter the uppercase or special characters.

Syntax

StringUpper("String")

Parameters

String- It denotes the string which you need to convert into uppercase letters.

Example 11.3

```
1    ;Declare and initializing variables
2    Local $mystring="### Hello World ! This is my Second String #####"
3
4    ;convert it to upper case using string function
5    $convt=StringUpper($mystring)
6
7    ;Displaying it
8    MsgBox(0,"Convert"," String after converision become "&$convt)
9
10
```

Fig 11.5 StringUpper function

As I did for the lowercase function, here also I declared a variable and assigned a string "### Hello World ! This is my Second String #####" to it. Convert it into uppercase using StringUpper function and assign it to a variable $convt. Finally display the output in the message box.

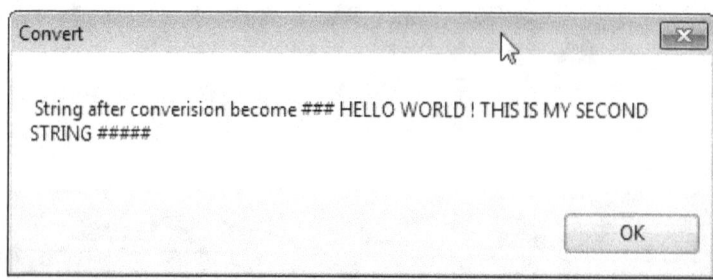

Fig 11.6 Output

StringIsUpper

This function returns true if the string contains only uppercase letter(s) and in all other cases like whitespaces, digits and special characters it returns false.

Syntax

StringIsUpper("String")

Parameters

String-It denotes the string to evaluate

Example 11.4

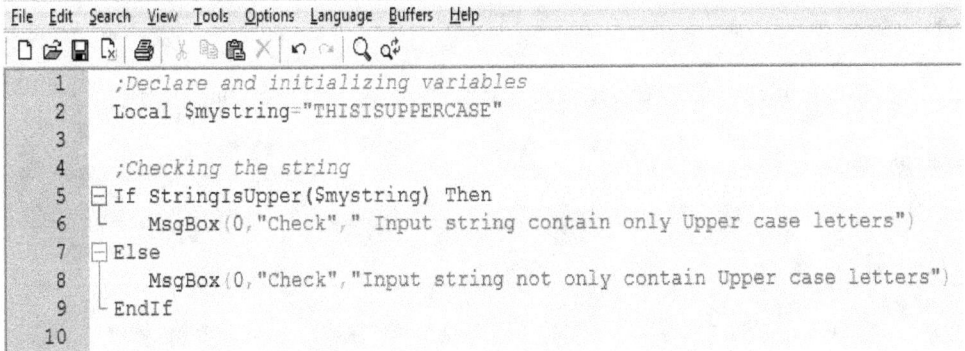

Fig 11.7 StringIsUpper function

String "THISISUPPERCASE" contains only uppercase, so the function StringIsUpper returns true.

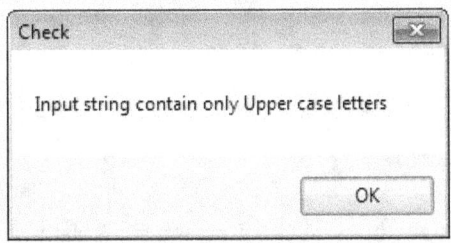

Fig 11.8 Output

StringLen

This function is used to determine the number of characters in a string. Apart from alphabetical characters, this function considers white spaces, symbols and digits for determining the string length.

Syntax

StringLen("String")

Parameters

String- It denotes the string which you need to determine its number of characters

Example 11.5

```
File Edit Search View Tools Options Language Buffers Help
 1      ;Declare and initializing variables
 2      Local $mystring="### Hello World ! What is going on?"
 3
 4      ;calcuating number of characters
 5      $num=StringLen($mystring)
 6
 7      ;Displaying it
 8      MsgBox(0,"Length"," Number of charcters in string is "&$num)
 9
10
```

Fig 11.9 StringLen function

The variable $mystring is passed as an argument to the function StringLen and it calculates the number of characters in the variable and assigns it to the variable $num. Finally, the msgbox function displays the output.

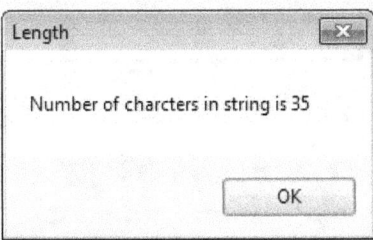

Fig 11.10 Output

StringIsDigit

This function returns true if it contains only numbers (0-9) and in all other cases such as white spaces, alphabetical characters and special characters it returns false.

Syntax

StringIsDigit("String")

Parameters

String-It denotes the string to evaluate

Example 11.6

```
File  Edit  Search  View  Tools  Options  Language  Buffers  Help

  1      ;Declare and initializing variables
  2      Local $string1="123John"
  3      Local $string2="100.00+20"
  4      Local $string3="$40"
  5      Local $string4="10030"
  6
  7      ;Checking digits
  8      $str1=StringIsDigit($string1)
  9      $str2=StringIsDigit($string2)
 10      $str3=StringIsDigit($string3)
 11      $str4=StringIsDigit($string4)
 12
 13      ;Displying output
 14      MsgBox(0,"Digit check","String 1returns "&$str1&@CRLF _
 15      &"String 2 returns "&$str2&@CRLF&"String 3 returns "&$str3&@CRLF _
 16      "String 4 returns "&$str4)
 17
 18
 19
```

Fig 11.11 StringIsDigitfucntion

The variable $str1 holds the value "123John," which contains both numbers and alphabetical characters so it returns false. The variable $str2 holds the value "100.00+20" which contains numbers and symbols, so it returns false. The variable $str3 holds "$40" which contains special characters and numbers, so it also returns false.Lastly, the variable $str4 holds "10030" which contains only numbers, so it returns true.

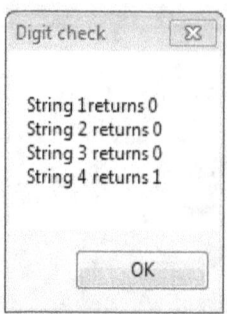

Fig 11.12 Output

StringLeft

This function is used to return substring with a specified number of characters from the main string starting from the left. It considers white spaces, alphabetical characters and special characters as characters.

Syntax

StringLeft ("String", count)

Parameters

String-It denotes the string to evaluate

Count-It denotes the number of characters to get from the main string

Example 11.7

```
File Edit Search View Tools Options Language Buffers Help

1      ;Declare and initializing variables
2      Local $string1="Could you please tell me your name?"
3
4      ;Get string
5      $str1=StringLeft($string1,11)
6
7      ;Displyaing output
8      MsgBox(0,"String functions","StringLeft function return  "&$str1)
```

Fig 11.13 StringLeftfucntion

Statement $str1=StringLeft($string1,11) gets the first 11 leftmost characters from $string1 and assigns them to variable $str1. It displays the 11 left most characters (9 alphabetical characters and 2 whitespaces) in the message box as shown below.

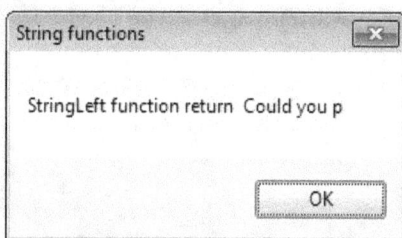

String functions

StringLeft function return Could you p

OK

Fig 11.14 Output

StringRight

This function returns substring with a specified number of characters from the main string starting from the right. In other words, it returns the specified characters from the end of a main string. It takes white spaces, alphabetical characters and special characters as characters.

Syntax

StringRight("String", count)

Parameters

String-It denotes the string to evaluate

Count-It denotes the number of characters to get from the main string

Example 11.8

```
1      ;Declare and initializing variables
2      Local $string1="Could you please tell me your name?"
3
4      ;Get string
5      $str1=StringRight($string1,11)
6
7      ;Displaying output
8      MsgBox(0,"String functions","StringRight function return  "&$str1)
```

Fig 11.15 StringRight function

I altered stringLeft with StringRight in the previous example. It returns 11 characters from the end or from the right hand side of the string.

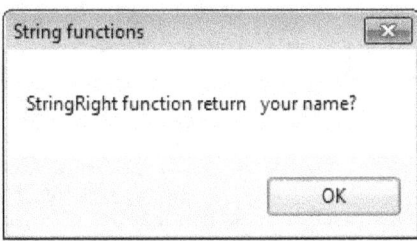

Fig 11.16 Output

StringMid

This returns the substring with a given number of characters present after the given position. It considers white spaces, alphabetical characters and special characters as characters.

Syntax

StringMid("String", start, [count])

Parameters

String-It denotes the string to evaluate

Start- It indicates the position to start extracting the sub string

Count (optional)-It denotes the number of characters to get from the main string

Note: If start exceeds the maximum number of characters in the string then it returns an empty string. If count exceeds the maximum number of characters in string then it return entire body of characters present after the start position

Example 11.9

```
File Edit Search View Tools Options Language Buffers Help
1    ;Declare and initializing variables
2    Local $string1="I'm going to extract characters from middle"
3
4    ;Get string
5    $str1=StringMid($string1,14,18)
6
7    ;Displyaing output
8    MsgBox(0,"String functions","StringMid funcition return ┤ "&$str1)
```

Fig 11.17 StringMid Function

StringMid ($string1,14,18)- This statement extracts 18 characters starting from the 14th position of the $string1 and assigns it to $str1.

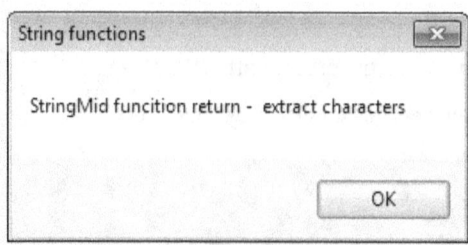

String functions

StringMid funcition return - extract characters

OK

Fig 11.18 Output

StringInStr

This function is used to search whether or not the given substring is present in the main string. It returns an integer which specifies the position of the given number of occurrences of the sub string in the main string.

Syntax

StringInStr("String", "Substring", [case sense], [Occurrence], [start],[Count])

Parameters

String-It denotes the string to evaluate

Substring- It denotes the string to find

Case sense (Optional)- It indicates whether the search should be case sensitive or insensitive. By default the value is 0.

0-This value performs a case insensitive search

1-This value performs a case sensitive search

2- This value performs a case insensitive search but faster than 0.

Occurrence (Optional)- It denotes which occurrence of the substring to find in the main string. Default value is 1 to find the first occurrence of the sub string. Negative value can be used to search from the reverse order.

Start- It indicates the position to start extracting the sub string. Default value is 1.

Count (optional)-It denotes the number of characters to search within the main string.

Note: Sub string should lie within the count value. Otherwise it returns 0.

Example 11.10

```
File  Edit  Search  View  Tools  Options  Language  Buffers  Help

  1
  2        ;Declare and initializing variables
  3        Local $string1="I'm going to get Some cHaRaCters from this get string"
  4
  5        ;Get position
  6
  7        $str1=StringInStr($string1,"to")
  8        $str2=StringInStr($string1," characters",1,1,7,40)
  9        $str3=StringInStr($string1,"cHaRaCters",1,1,5,50)
 10        $str4=StringInStr($string1,"get",0,2,1,47)
 11
 12        ;Displaying output
 13        MsgBox(0,"String functions","String 1 Return "&$str1&
 14        @CRLF&"String 2 Return "&$str2&@CRLF&"String 3 Return "&$str3&
 15        @CRLF&"String 4 Return "&$str4)
```

Fig 11.19 StringInStr function

$str1

StringInStr ($string1,"to")- This simple statement finds the word "to" from the main string $string1 and returns the position of the first occurrence of the word "to" by starting to count its position from the left.

$str2

StringInStr($string1," characters",1,1,7,40)- This statement searches for a case sensitive word "characters" within $string1 since we set the case sense parameter as 1. Here it returns 0 because the case sensitive match for a word "characters" is not found. The fourth argument is 1, so it returns the position of the first occurrence of the word "characters" from the left. The fifth argument contains the value 7 so it starts searching the character from the 7th position of the main string $string1 from the left. The sixth argument contains the value 40, so it searches the word "characters" within the first 40 characters.

$sstr3

StringInStr($string1,"cHaRaCters",1,1,5,50)- This statement also searches for a case sensitive word "cHaRaCters" within $string1 since we set the case sense parameter as 1. If found, it returns the position or else returns 0.

$str4

StringInStr($string1,"get",0,2,1,47)- This statement searches for the word "get" and returns the second occurrence position since the occurrence value is 2.

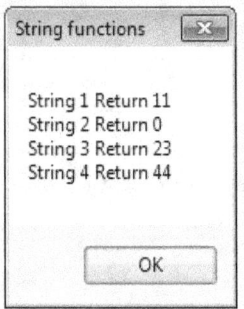

String functions

String 1 Return 11
String 2 Return 0
String 3 Return 23
String 4 Return 44

OK

Fig 11.20 Output

StringReverse

This function returns the given string in the reverse order.

Syntax

StringReverse("string",[Flag])

Parameters

String-It denotes the string to evaluate

Flag (Optional) - It indicates the way it returns. It accepts two values 0 and 1. 0 returns the reverse string by default method and 1 returns the result in a faster way.

Example 11.11

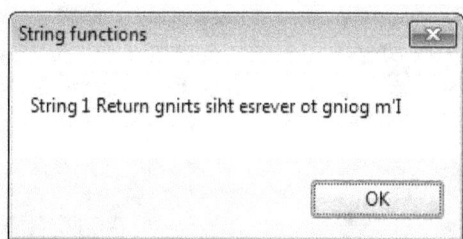

```
1
2      ;Declare and initializing variables
3      Local $string1="I'm going to reverse this string"
4
5      ;reverse the string
6
7      $str1=StringReverse($string1,1)
8
9      ;Displyaing output
10     MsgBox(0,"String functions","String 1 Return "&$str1)
```

Fig 11.21 StringReverse function

StringReverse($string1,1) – Statement returns the reverse of the $string1 from right to left and assigns it to $str1.

String functions

String 1 Return gnirts siht esrever ot gniog m'I

OK

Fig 11.22 Output

String Replace

It replaces the character(s) present in the main string with given characters.

Syntax

StringReplace ("string","String to be replaced or position of string"," replace string", [occurrence], [case sense])

Parameters

String-It denotes the string to evaluate

String to be replaced or its position- It accepts two different types of values. You can either give the "String you want to be replaced" or the character position of the string to be replaced from the left.

Replace string- It denotes the replacement string

Occurrence (Optional)- It indicates the number of times it should replace the string if the string to be replaced appears in the main string multiple times. You should ignore this parameter when you give the position of the string in the second argument. By default it replaces all the strings.

Case sense- It indicates whether the replacement should be case sensitive or insensitive. By default the value is 0.

0-This value performs a case insensitive search

1-This value performs a case sensitive search

2- This value performs a case insensitive search but faster than 0.

You should ignore this parameter when you give the position of the string in the second argument.

Example 11.12

```
File  Edit  Search  View  Tools  Options  Language  Buffers  Help

  D ☞ 🖫 🖫 | 🖨 | ⅄ 🖺 🖺 ✕ | ↻ ↺ | 🔍 🔍⁺

    1
    2      ;Declare and initializing variables
    3      Local $string1="Hello Hi hello Hi Hello Hi Hello hi "
    4
    5      ;replcaing the string
    6
    7      $str1=StringReplace($string1,"Hi","Hello",0,0)
    8      $str2=StringReplace($string1,"Hello","Hi",2,1)
    9      $str3=StringReplace($string1,7,"bi")
   10
   11
   12      ;Displyaing output
   13      MsgBox(0,"String functions","String 1 Return "&$str1& _
   14      @CRLF&"String  2 Return "&$str2&@CRLF&"String  3 Return "&$str3)
```

Fig 11.23 StringReplace function

$str1

StringReplace($string1,"Hi","Hello",0,0)- This statement replaces all instances of "Hi" with "Hello" because its case sense is 0 and occurrence is also given as 0.

$str2

StringReplace($string1,"Hello","Hi",2,1)- This statement replaces "Hello" with "Hi" for the first two occurrences with a case sensitive match. It replaces the first and third "Hello" with "Hi" because the second occurrence of "hello" fails the case sense match.

$str3

StringReplace($string1,7,"byee")- This statement replaces the character present in the 7th position with "byee," but be conscious that unlike replacement, it won't replace the previous string with the given string. Instead, it will start appending the given characters from the given position. So, it will overlap the existing string with new string.

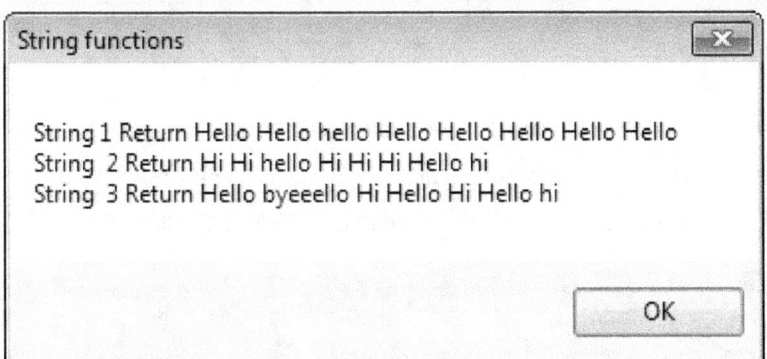

Fig 11.24 Output

12) Windows functions

All the window based applicationshavetheir own window names, titles, properties and controls. To automate a window based application, we need to identify its name, title, properties and controls with the help of the AutoIT window info tool. Once it is identified, we can easily automate our task. AutoIT has several window functions to handle multiple windows in a single script. Let's look at those functions and their uses in detail.

WinActivate

This function is used to activate the window if it's in a minimized state.If multiple windows are opened in the screen, then it gives focus to the particular window by identifying its handle. This function will work only if the window is already launched or else it will return 0.

Syntax

WinActivate ("Title", [Text])

Parameters

Title- It defines the title/ handle/ class of the window to activate

Text (Optional)- It indicates the text identified by the AutoIt window info tool

In order to activate the currently active window, you can use WinActivate("[ACTIVE]"). The Parameter [ACTIVE] can be used for any window function to get the control of the currently active window.

Note: If multiple windows have the same title and text, then it activates the most recently active window.

Example 12.1

To activate the calculator, we need to get the calculator title and text (optional) by using the AutoIT window info tool. Place the finder tool on the calculator window as shown in the below

Fig. to capture the title. It's recommended that you copy the title from the Finder tool because the window title is case sensitive. The calculator window doesn't have any text, so we are going to activate it with title alone. Launch the calculator and minimize it before executing the script. When the script is compiled, it will activate the calculator.

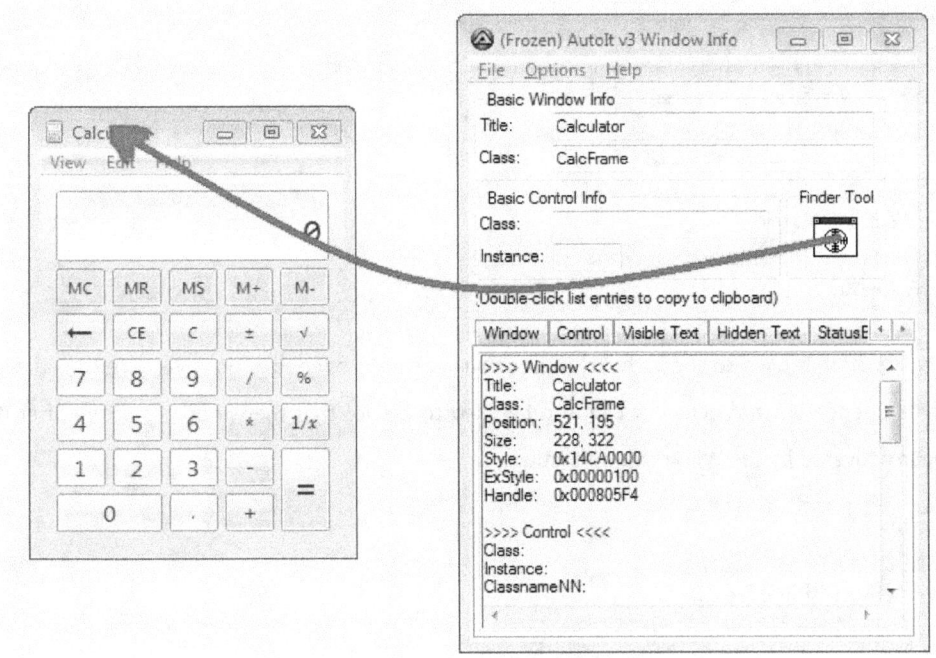

Fig 12.1 Finder tool finding properties of calculator

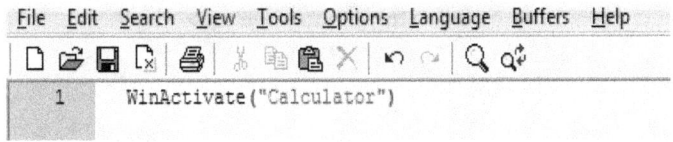

Fig 12.2 Winactivate function

After compiling the script, the calculator window will be launched.

Fig 12.3 Calculator

WinActive

This function is used to check that the specified window is opened and active. It returns 0 even if it's opened but not active. It can also be used to ensure that the window is active after it's been activated by the WinActivate function.

Syntax

WinActive ("Title", [Text])

Parameters

Title- It defines the title/ handle/ class of the window to activate

Text (Optional)- It indicates the text identified by the AutoIt window info tool

Example 12.2

I'm going to activate the calculator window with theWinActivate function and verify whether it's currently active after it's been activated by the WinActive function. But before compiling, you should open and minimize the calculator window.

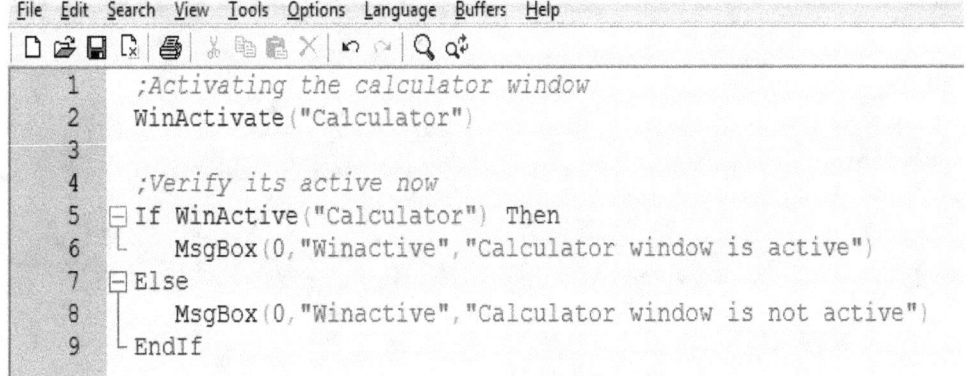

```
1      ;Activating the calculator window
2      WinActivate("Calculator")
3
4      ;Verify its active now
5    ⊟ If WinActive("Calculator") Then
6    └    MsgBox(0,"Winactive","Calculator window is active")
7    ⊟ Else
8    |     MsgBox(0,"Winactive","Calculator window is not active")
9    └ EndIf
```

Fig 12.4 WinActive function

When compiling, the calculator window will be activated and theWinActive Function will check whether the calculator window is active.If it's active, then it will display the message "Calculator window is active." Output is shown below:

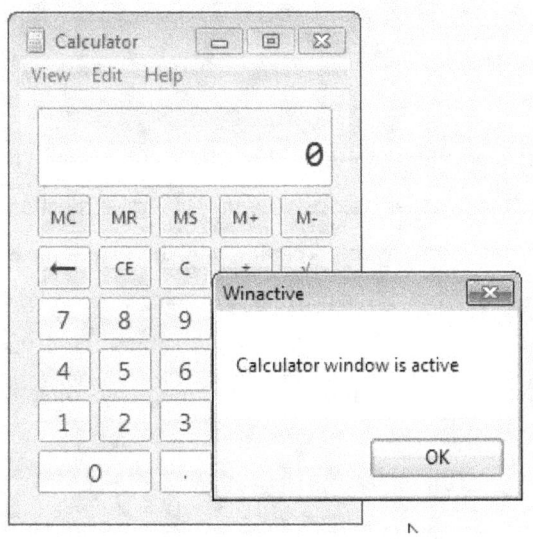

Fig 12.5 Output

WinClose

This function is used to close the window.

Syntax

WinClose ("Title", [Text])

Parameters

Title- It defines the title/ handle/ class of the window to activate

Text (Optional)- It indicates the text identified by the AutoIt window info tool

Note: If multiple windows have same title and text then it closes the most recently active window.

Example 12.3

I'm going to launch the calculator by Run command, then using the WinClose function, I'm going to close the calculator window and ensure whether it's closed by the WinActive function. In the Run command, you need to specify the name of the program with the extension to launch it. You can get those details from the properties of the program. I'm going to show how to get the name and extension of the calculator. Type "calc" in the start button, and the calculator will be listed.Right click the calculator and select properties. The properties window will be launched as shown in the Fig.

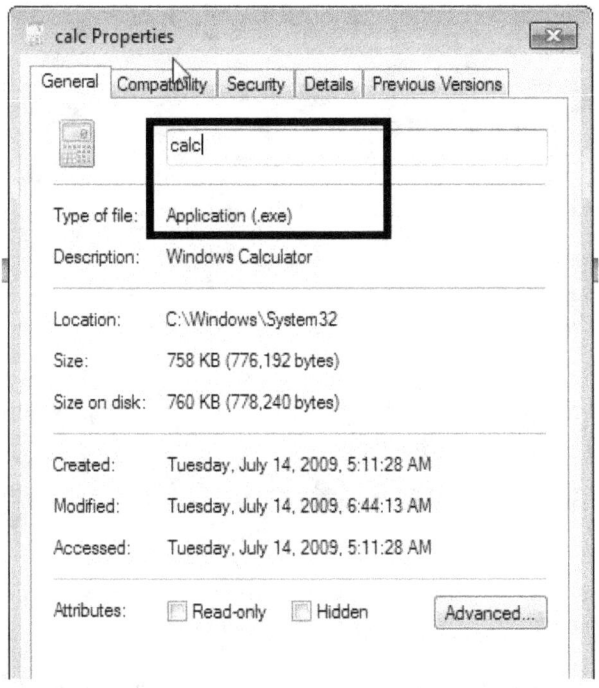

Fig 12.6 Calculator properties window

The calculator name and extension are highlighted within the box in the figure above. We should pass "calc.exe" as a parameter to Runthe command. Here, we used the sleep function to pause the script for 2 seconds. The reason behind this is that even though the script controls the processor,launching the calculator will take a few seconds.This also depends on the speed and performance of your processor.During this time script, move on to the next line and start compiling it. When executing the script, the calculator window will be launched. The winactivate function activates the calculator and the winactive ensures the calculator window is active.If it's active, it will close the Calculator.

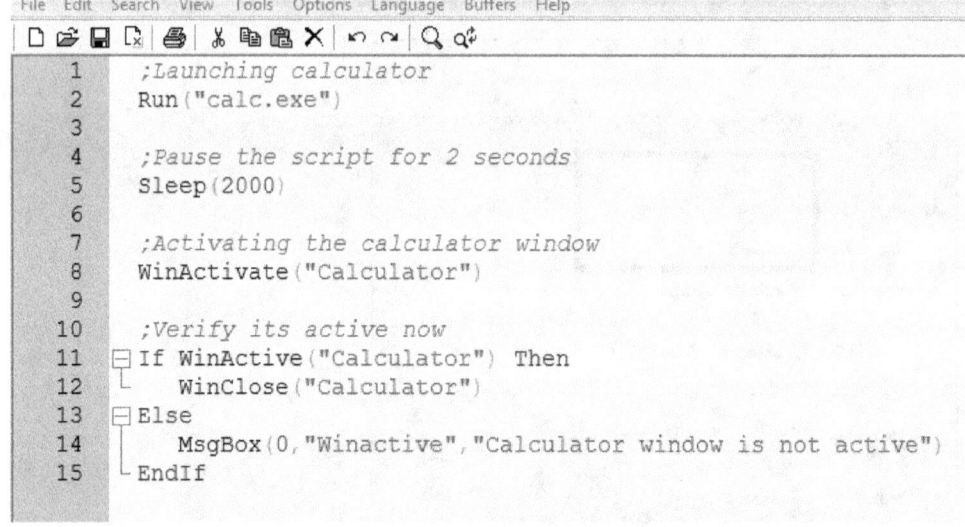

```
 1    ;Launching calculator
 2    Run("calc.exe")
 3
 4    ;Pause the script for 2 seconds
 5    Sleep(2000)
 6
 7    ;Activating the calculator window
 8    WinActivate("Calculator")
 9
10    ;Verify its active now
11   ⊟If WinActive("Calculator") Then
12    └    WinClose("Calculator")
13   ⊟Else
14    │    MsgBox(0,"Winactive","Calculator window is not active")
15    └EndIf
```

Fig 12.7 WinClosefucntion

WinExists

This function checks whether or not the specified window exists. It returns true even when the window is launched and it's in a minimized or hidden state. It will return false only when the window does not exist.

Syntax

WinExists ("Title", [Text])

Parameters

Title- It defines the title/ handle/ class of the window to activate

Text (Optional)- It indicates the text identified by the AutoIt window info tool

Example 12.4

```
     1
     2     ;Verify its exists
     3   ┌ If WinExists("Calculator") Then
     4   └     WiMsgBox(0,"Winactive","Calculator window is exist")
     5   ┌ Else
     6   │     MsgBox(0,"Winactive","Calculator window is not exist")
     7   └ EndIf
```

Fig 12.8 WinExists function

Before compiling the above script, I launched calculator and kept it in a minimized state. I checked the existence of the calculator with the above script and it returns true. So, the msgbox displayed "Calculator window is exist."

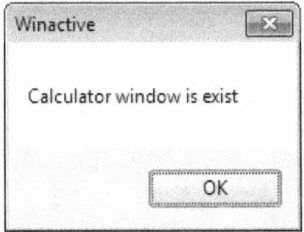

Fig 12.9 Output

WinGetClassList

This function is used to get the list of classes from a specified window. It automatically inserts linefeed to all classes while displaying, and it has the capacity to store 64kb of text. If more than one window matches the window title and text then it returns the class of the most recently activated window.

Syntax

WinGetClassList ("Title", [Text])

Parameters

Title- It defines the title/ handle/ class of the window to activate

Text (Optional)- It indicates the text identified by the AutoIt window info tool

Example 12.5

```autoit
File  Edit  Search  View  Tools  Options  Language  Buffers  Help

1    ;Launching calculator window
2    Run ("Calc.exe")
3
4    ;Pause script for launching of calculator window
5    Sleep (2000)
6
7    ;Get the window class list
8    $list=WinGetClassList ("Calculator")
9
10   ;Displaying the list of classes
11   MsgBox (0, "Calculator classes", $list)
```

Fig 12.10 WinGetClassList function

In the example above, the script will launch the calculator and pause the script for 2 seconds to launch. WinGetClassList gets the list of classes in the Calculator window and assigns it to the variable $list. Finally, the list of classes is displayed in the msgbox with an automatic line feed.

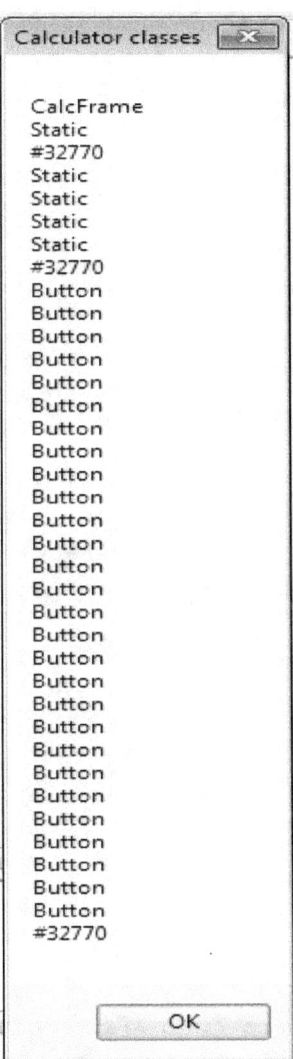

Fig 12.11 Output

WinGetHandle

This function is used to get the internal handle of the window. One of the advantages of this function is you can use this handle for all of the window functions instead of specifying its title.

Syntax

WinGetHandle ("Title", [Text])

Parameters

Title- It defines the title/ handle/ class of the window to activate

Text (Optional)- It indicates the text identified by the AutoIt window info tool

Example 12.6

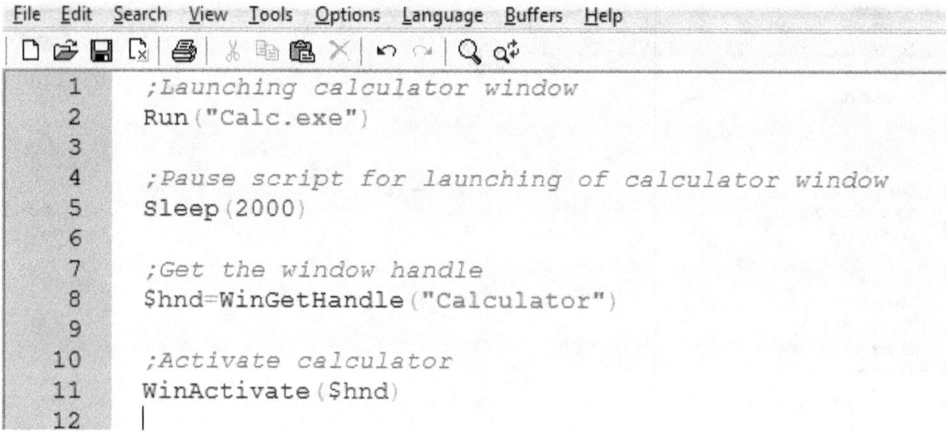

```
File  Edit  Search  View  Tools  Options  Language  Buffers  Help

1        ;Launching calculator window
2        Run("Calc.exe")
3
4        ;Pause script for launching of calculator window
5        Sleep(2000)
6
7        ;Get the window handle
8        $hnd=WinGetHandle("Calculator")
9
10       ;Activate calculator
11       WinActivate($hnd)
12       |
```

Fig 12.12 WinGetHandle function

In the above example, the WinGetHandle function gets the handle of the calculator and assigns it to the variable $hnd. The WinActivate function uses the handle to activate the calculator instead of title and text. Finally,the calculator window will be launched and activated.

Fig 12.13 Output

WinGetState

This function is used to get the state such as minimized, maximized, active etc. of the specified window and return a corresponding integer value.(Refer to the table below). Sometimes multiple return values are added together and displayed.

Syntax

WinGetState ("Title", [Text])

Parameters

Title- It defines the title/ handle/ class of the window to activate

Text (Optional)- It indicates the text identified by the AutoIt window info tool

Table 12.1 Window state

Example 12.7

```
File  Edit  Search  View  Tools  Options  Language  Buffers  Help

1      ;Launching calculator window
2      Run("calc.exe")
3
4      ;Pause script for launching of calculator window
5      Sleep(2000)
6
7      ;Get the window state
8      $stat=WinGetState("Calculator","")
9
10     MsgBox(0,"Window state",$stat)
```

Fig 12.14 WinGetState function

Value of WinGetState is assigned to the variable $stat and displayed in the msgbox.

Window state
15
OK

Fig 12.15 Output

The value returned by the WinGetState function is 15, which is the sum of (1+2+4+8). This indicates that the window exists, is visible and is enabled and active.

WinGetTitle

This function is used to get the title of the window. It will retrieve the title even when the window is hidden or minimized.

Syntax

WinGetTitle ("Title", [Text])

Parameters

Title- It defines the title/ handle/ class of the window to activate

Text (Optional) - It indicates the text identified by the AutoIt window info tool

Example 12.8

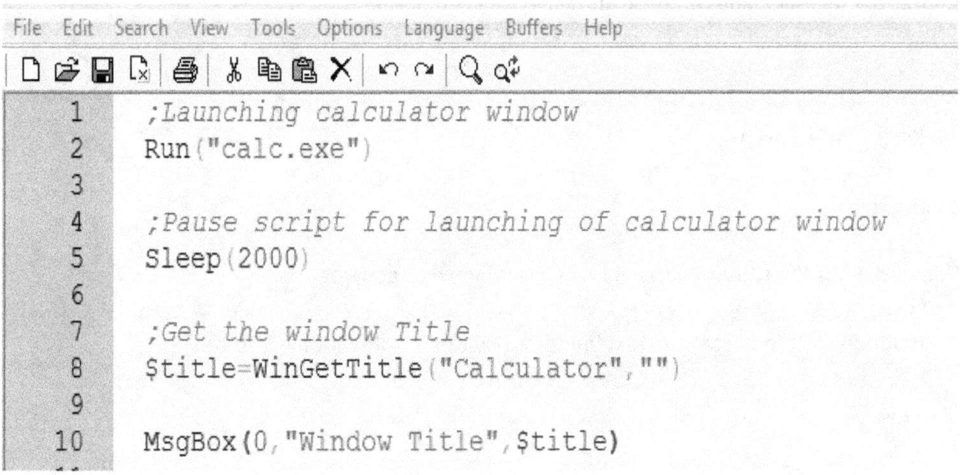

```
File  Edit  Search  View  Tools  Options  Language  Buffers  Help

1     ;Launching calculator window
2     Run("calc.exe")
3
4     ;Pause script for launching of calculator window
5     Sleep(2000)
6
7     ;Get the window Title
8     $title=WinGetTitle("Calculator","")
9
10    MsgBox(0,"Window Title",$title)
```

Fig 12.16 WinGetTitle function

Upon executing this script, it will launch the Calculator window. The function WinGetTitle gets the title of the calculator and assigns it to the variable $title and it's displayed using the msgbox function.

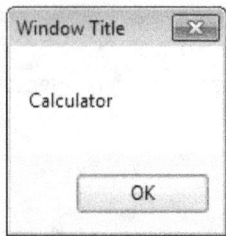

Fig 12.17 Output

WinKill

This function is used to force-close a specified window. The difference between WinClose and WinKill is that when closing the window using WinClose, some windows will display a prompt message like "Do you want to save?" The notepad window does this, for example, but WinKill ignores the message and force-closes it.

Syntax

WinKill ("Title", [Text])

Parameters

Title- It defines the title/ handle/ class of the window to activate

Text (Optional)- It indicates the text identified by the AutoIt window info tool

Example 12.9

Now I'm going to show the difference between the WinClose and WinKill using the notepad application. As I already mentioned, you need to find the name and extension of the application from the properties window. In my computer, the name and extension of the notepad window are "notepad.exe" which I'm going to give as a parameter for the Run command to launch a new notepad window. Then I need to find the window title and text (if any) of the untitled notepad window with AutoIt window info tool as shown in the Fig. You should open a new notepad and find this before writing the script.Close it after finding its title and text.

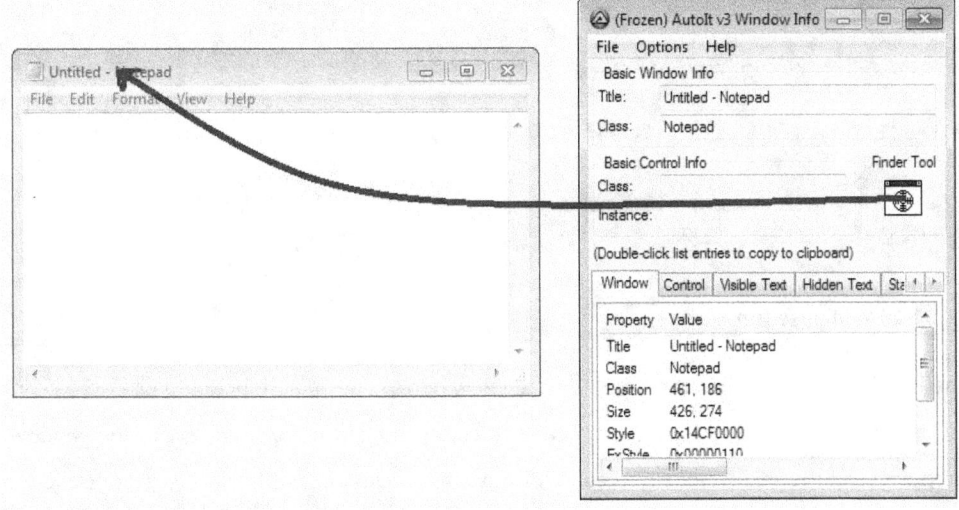

Fig 12.18 Finding properties of Untitled- Notepad

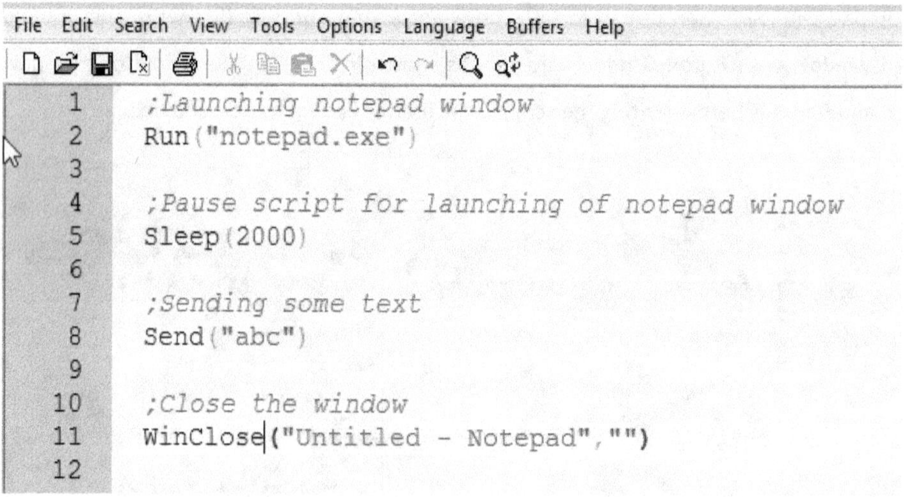

```
1    ;Launching notepad window
2    Run("notepad.exe")
3
4    ;Pause script for launching of notepad window
5    Sleep(2000)
6
7    ;Sending some text
8    Send("abc")
9
10   ;Close the window
11   WinClose("Untitled - Notepad","")
12
```

Fig 12.19 WinClose function

The Run function launches the untitled notepad window. The sleep function pauses the script for 2 seconds to launch the notepad. The send command is used to send text to the window. Here we send the text "abc" to notepad for a prompt message, and finally we try to close the notepad with the WinClose function. Do you think it will close?

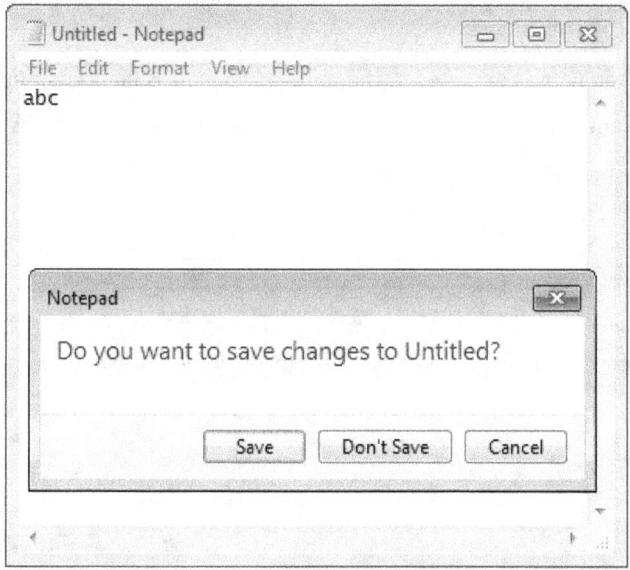

Fig 12.20 Output

When I executed the script, it entered text "abc" in the notepad and the WinClose function tried to close the notepad, but the prompt message stopped it from closing. The above Fig is the final output of the WinClose function.

```
1   ;Launching notepad window
2   Run("notepad.exe")
3
4   ;Pause script for launching of notepad window
5   Sleep(2000)
6
7   ;Sending some text
8   Send("abc")
9
10  ;Close the window
11  WinKill("Untitled - Notepad","")
12
```

Fig 12.21 WinKill function

I replace WinClose with WinKill, and when I executed it, the notepad window is launched, text "abc" is entered, and the prompt message "Do you want to save changed to Untitled Notepad?" is displayed.However, after a few seconds it is force closed.

WinMinimizeAll

This function is used to minimize all the maximized or visible windows and display the desktop. When multiple windows are opened, we can use this function to minimize all windows and activate only the ones we need.

Syntax

WinMinimizeAll()

No parameters required.

Example 12.10

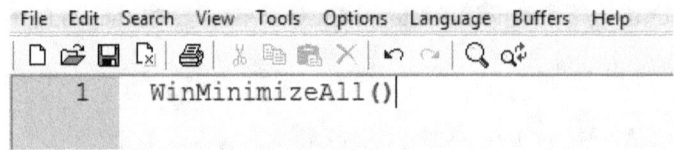

Fig 12.22 WinMinimizeAll function

When executing the above script, it minimizes all the windows and shows the desktop.

WinMinimizeAllUndo

This function reverses the WinMinimizeAll function.

Syntax

WinMinimizeAllUndo()

No parameters required.

Example 12.11

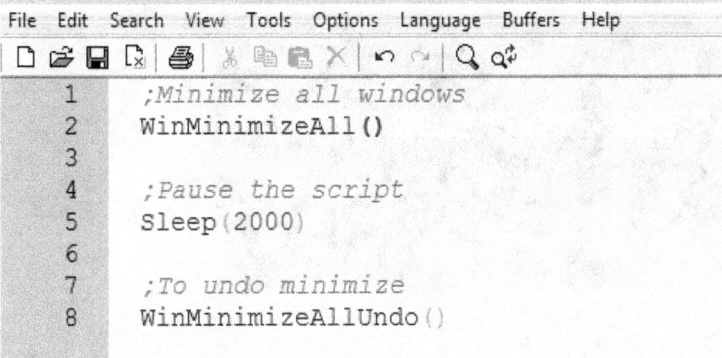

```
1    ;Minimize all windows
2    WinMinimizeAll()
3
4    ;Pause the script
5    Sleep(2000)
6
7    ;To undo minimize
8    WinMinimizeAllUndo()
```

Fig 12.23 WinMinimizeAllUndo function

When executing the script, it minimizes all open windows and shows the desktop screen for 2 seconds before reversing the minimize action for all windows.

WinSetState

This function is used to change the state of the specified window. When you want to maximize, minimize, enable, hide or show the window, then it can be done with the corresponding macro.

Syntax

WinSetState ("Title", "Text", Flag)

Parameters

Title- It defines the title/ handle/ class of the window to activate

Text- It indicates the text identified by the AutoIt window info tool

Note: text is mandatory here, so even though your window doesn't have text or you don't want to mention text, you must provide an empty string "".

Flag- It indicates the required state of the window. Refer to the table below:

Table 12.2 WinSetState Macro and its description

Example 12.12

```
1    ;Launch notepad
2    Run("notepad.exe")
3
4    ;Wait for 2 seconds
5    Sleep(2000)
6
7    ;Maximize the notepad window
8    WinSetState("Untitled - Notepad","",@SW_MAXIMIZE)
9    Sleep(2000)
10   ;Minimize the notepad window
11   WinSetState("Untitled - Notepad","",@SW_MINIMIZE)
12   Sleep(2000)
13   ;Hide the notepad window
14   WinSetState("Untitled - Notepad","",@SW_HIDE)
15   Sleep(2000)
16   ;Show the notepad window
17   WinSetState("Untitled - Notepad","",@SW_SHOW)
18
```

Fig 12.24 WinSetState function

First it launches the notepad window.The window will be launched with its default size, but two seconds later it will be maximized with the @SW_MAXIMIZE macro. Two seconds later it will be hidden with @SW_HIDE macro, and two seconds later it will show with @SW_SHOW macro. Take note that the @SW_SHOW macro doesn't activate the notepad window and keeps it in a minimized state, but won't hide it.

WinWait

This function is used to pause the script for a given time until the specified window exists. It will return true even when the window is in a minimized or hidden state. When launching some applications, it will take a few minutes to show on the screen, so we can use the WinWait function to wait for a specified time until the specified window is launched. The difference between the Sleep and WinWait is that the sleep function simply pauses the script for a specified time and resumes when the time passes. Using WinWait, we are able to determine whether the specified window is launched or not.

Syntax

WinWait ("Title", [Text, Time Out])

Parameters

Title- It defines the title/ handle/ class of the window to activate

Text (Optional)- It indicates the text identified by the AutoIt window info tool

Time out (Optional) - It indicates the time to wait for window to appear

Note: Default time out is 0 seconds.

Example 12.13

```
File  Edit  Search  View  Tools  Options  Language  Buffers  Help

  1      ;It will Wait 4 seconds for notepad to appear
  2
  3    ⊟ If WinWait("Untitled - Notepad","",4) Then
  4          MsgBox(0,"Notepad", "Notepad window is succefully appeared")
  5    ⊟ Else
  6          MsgBox(0,"Notepad", "Notepad window is Not appeared")
  7    └ EndIf
  8
```

Fig 12.25 WinWait function

In the above script, I neither launch notepad previously nor in the script, so in this case the WinWait function waits for 4 seconds and checks the existence of the notepad window and returns false.

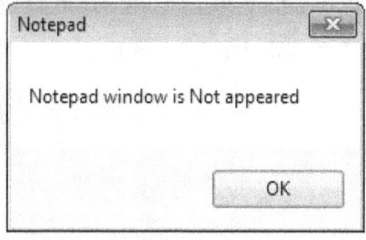

Fig 12.26 Output

WinWaitActive

This function pauses the script until the specified window is active. The difference between the WinWait and WinWaitActive is that WinWait checks only for the existence (maximize, minimize or hidden) while WinWaitActive actively checks whether or not the window is active. It returns true only if the window is currently active and in all other cases it returns false.

Syntax

WinWaitActive ("Title", [Text, Time Out])

Parameters

Title- It defines the title/ handle/ class of the window to activate

Text (Optional) - It indicates the text identified by the AutoIt window info tool

Time out(Optional)- It indicates the time to wait for window to appear

Note: Default time out is 0 seconds.

Example 12.14

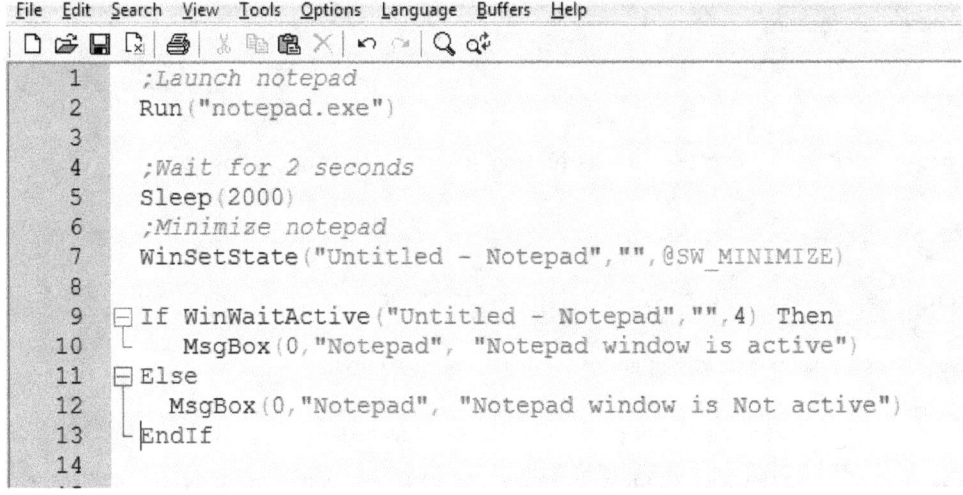

```
     File  Edit  Search  View  Tools  Options  Language  Buffers  Help

     1      ;Launch notepad
     2      Run("notepad.exe")
     3
     4      ;Wait for 2 seconds
     5      Sleep(2000)
     6      ;Minimize notepad
     7      WinSetState("Untitled - Notepad","",@SW_MINIMIZE)
     8
     9      If WinWaitActive("Untitled - Notepad","",4) Then
    10          MsgBox(0,"Notepad", "Notepad window is active")
    11      Else
    12          MsgBox(0,"Notepad", "Notepad window is Not active")
    13      EndIf
    14
```

Fig 12.27 WinWaitActive function

In the above example, it will launch notepad, but 2 seconds later it minimizes it with the WinSetState function. Then, using WinWaitActive, it checks whether it's currently active or not. In this case, it's not active because it was minimized by the WinSetState function.

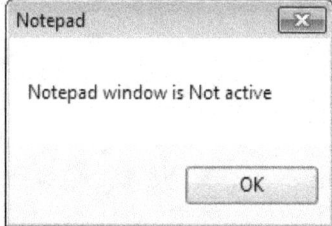

Fig 12.28 Output

Control Click

This function is used to simulate a mouse click on a specified control. It is very useful when we want to click specified controls such as buttons, textboxes, dropdown boxes, checkboxes etc. in window applications.

Syntax

ControlClick ("Title", "Text", Control ID, [Button, [Clicks, [X-Position, [Y-Position]]]])

Parameters

Title- It defines the title/ handle/ class of the window to activate

Text- It indicates the text identified by the AutoIt window info tool

Control ID- It indicates the numeric identifier that window assigns to each control. Here you can also specify properties such as Class, Instance, ClassNN, text, name, position and size. You can get all those names of the properties with the AutoIT window Info tool. Let's look at multiple ways of specifying it.

Case 1 Control ID

When you are going to specify control ID of control to click then you can specify the control ID as it is in the parameter.

ControlClick ("Calculator" ,"", 138) – Here 138 is the control ID of button 8 in Calculator

Case 2 Instance

When you are going to specify the instance of control to click then you need to define as shown below

ControlClick ("Calculator", "" ,"[INSTANCE:5]")- Here 5 is the instance of button 1 in Calculator

Case 3 Multiple Properties

When you are going to use multiple properties of control then it should be in the format below

[PROPERTY1:Value1; PROPERTY2:Value2]

Ex ControlClick("Calculator","" , "[CLASS:Button; INSTANCE:11; ID:132]")- This statement clicks button 2 in calculator.

Button (Optional)- It indicates the mouse button to click. By default it will click the "left" button. Use "right" to simulate right click and "middle" to simulate middle click.

Clicks (Optional) – It indicates the number of times to simulate the mouse click. By default it is 1. If you specify 2 then it performs a double click.

X- Position (Optional)- It indicates the X- coordinate to click within the control. By default it clicks at the center.

Y- Position (Optional)- It indicates the Y- coordinate to click within the control. By default it clicks at the center.

Example 12.15

I'm going to click button 9 in the calculator. To do this, I need to identify the properties of button 9. I can get that value by using the AutoIT window info tool.

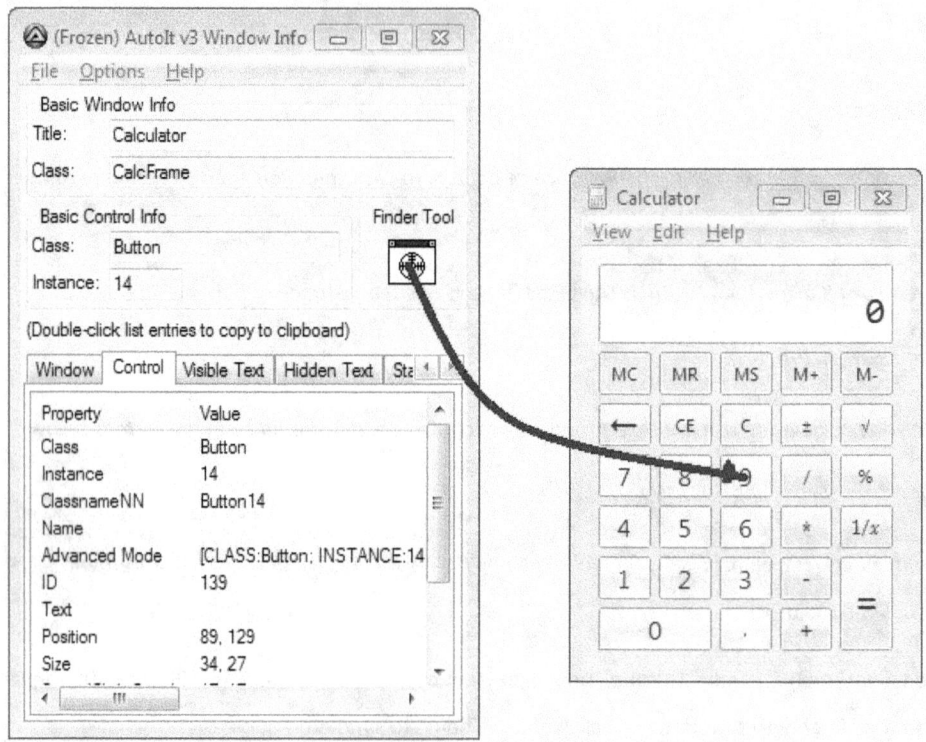

Fig 12.29 Finding the properties of calculator

I'm going to click button 9 by specifying Instance, Class and ID in the script. The value of Instance, Class and ID is 14, Button and 139 respectively from the AutoIT window Info tool.

```
File Edit Search View Tools Options Language Buffers Help
1    ;Launch calculator
2    Run("calc.exe")
3
4    ;Wait for 2 seconds
5    Sleep(2000)
6
7    ;Click the button 2
8    ControlClick("Calculator","","[ID:139; INSTANCE:14; CLASS:Button]")
```

Fig 12.30 ControlClick function

In the above example, I didn't include information about Clicks, buttons, or X and Y positions, so the default value should apply. When executing the script it will launch the calculator and click button 9.

Fig 12.31 Output

13) Calculator Automation

AutoIT is able to automate any window application. In this chapter I'm going to automate the calculator, which is one of the native window applications.

Task To Perform

What I really want to do is have the calculator multiply 84 and 40, divide the value by 2 and display the output.

When I click on the .exe file, it should launch the calculator window. Then, it should press the list of buttons below in the same order as I listed to perform my task.

1)It should press button 8

2)It should press button 4

3)It should press button *

4)It should press button 4

5)It should press button 0

6)It should press button =

7)It should press button /

8)It should press button 2

9)It should press button =

Pre-Requisite

I should know the properties such as Class, Instance and control ID of button 8,4,*,0,=,/,2 to press the corresponding button.

Let's determine the properties using the AutoIT window Info tool.

1) Properties of button 8

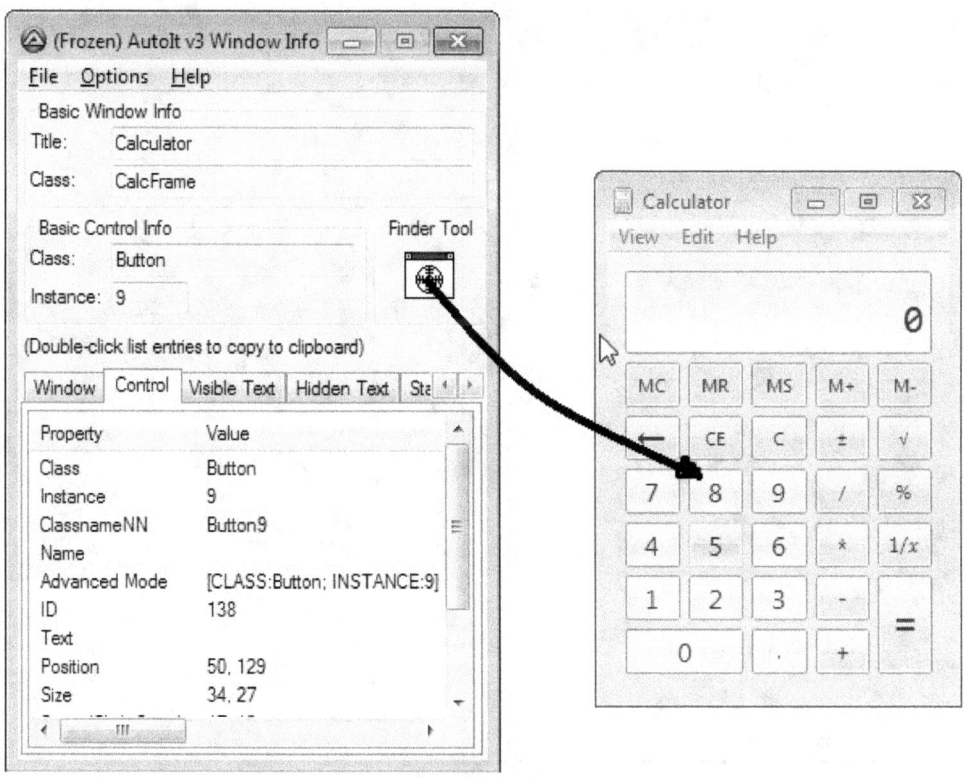

Fig 13.1 Properties of button 8

2) Properties of button 4

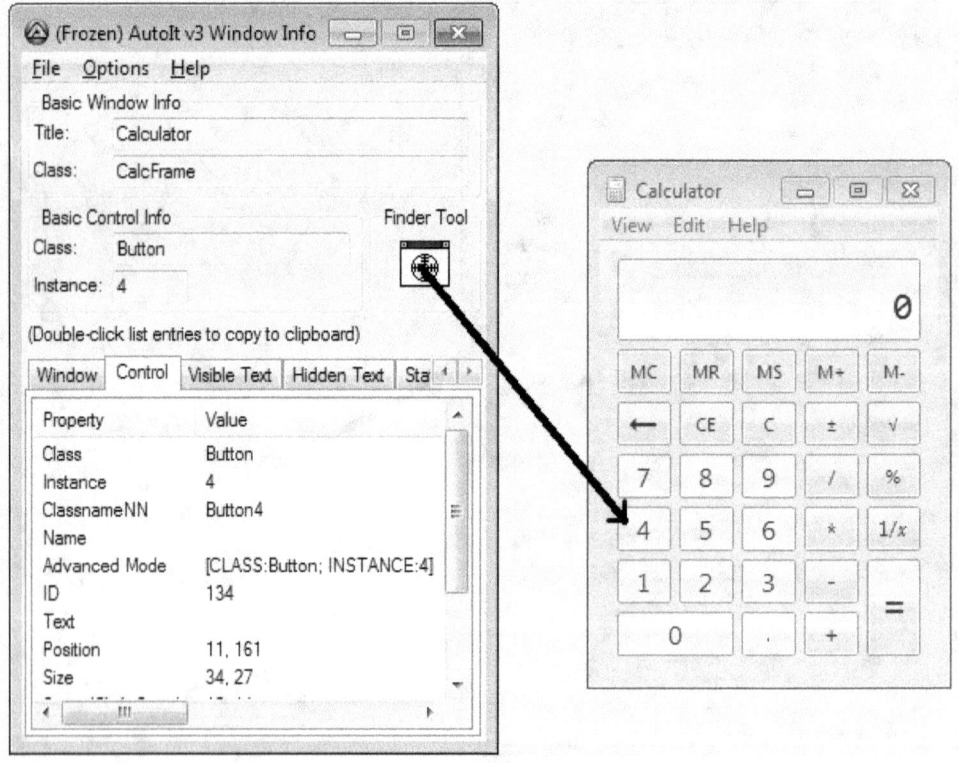

Fig 13.2Properties of button 4

3) Properties of button *

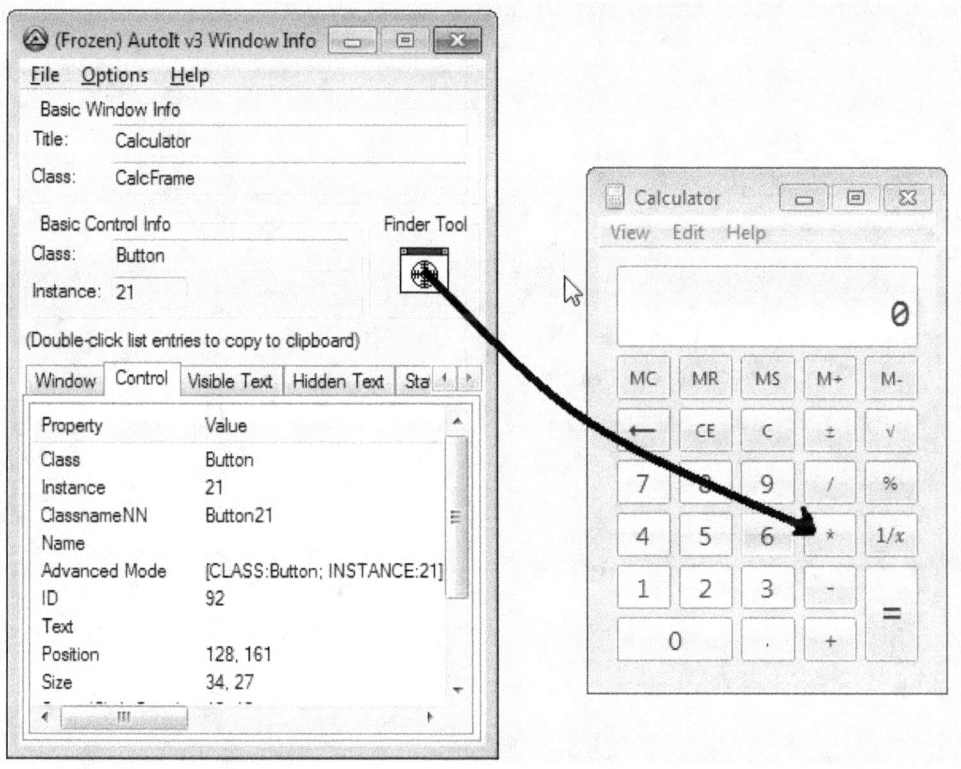

Fig 13.3Properties of button *

4) Properties of button 0

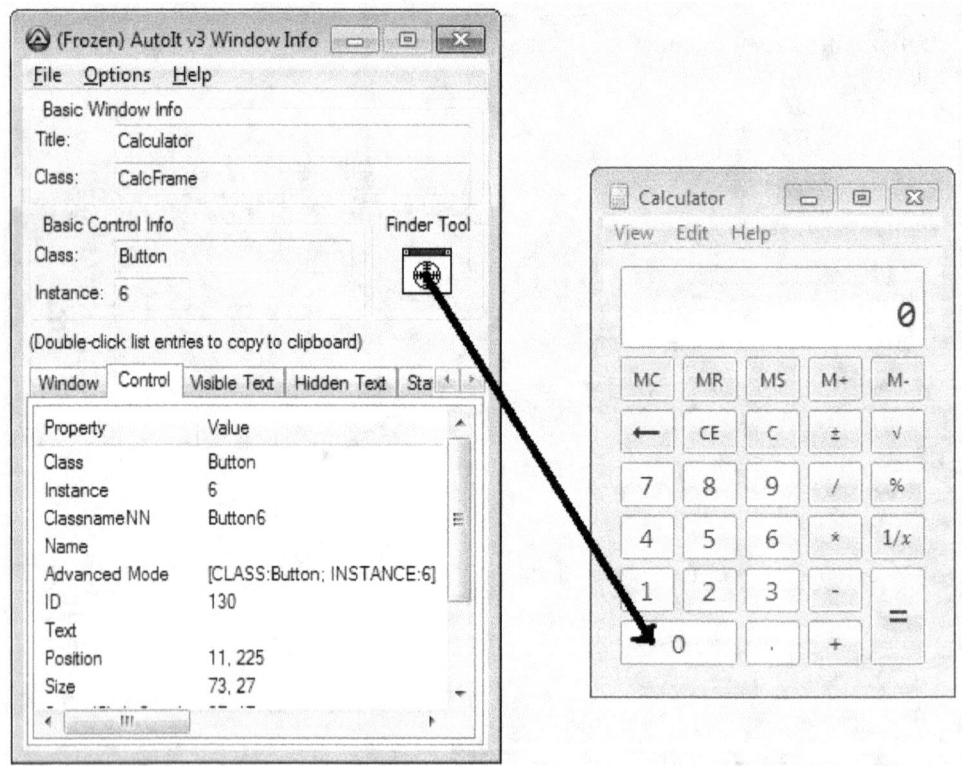

Fig 13.4Properties of button 0

5) Properties of button =

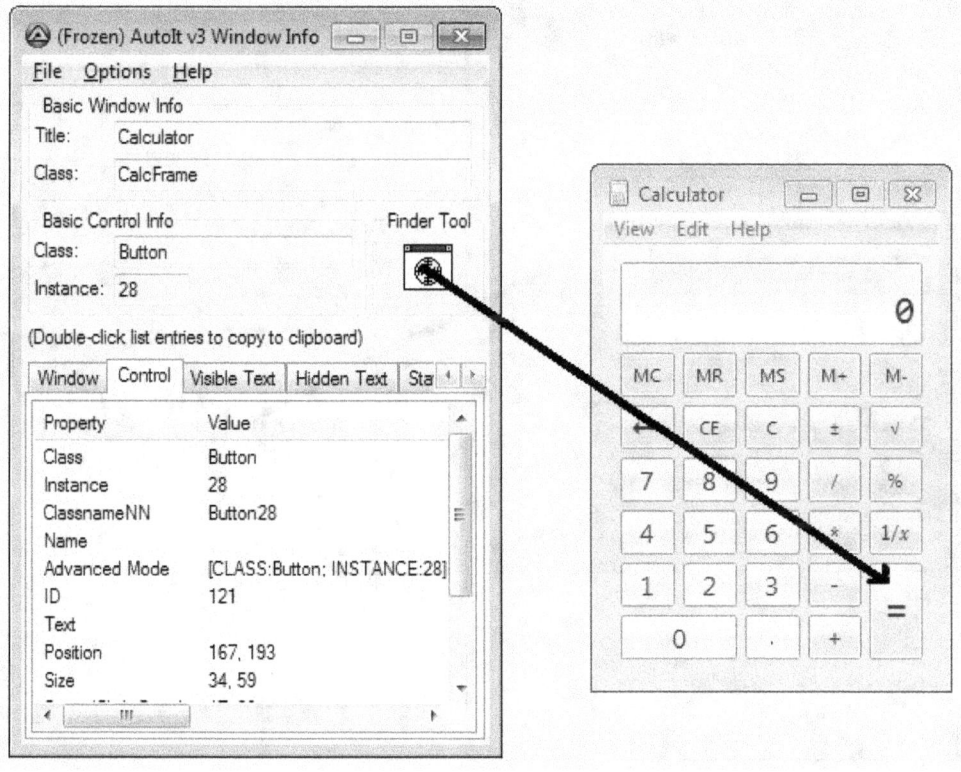

Fig 13.5 Properties of button =

6) Properties of button /

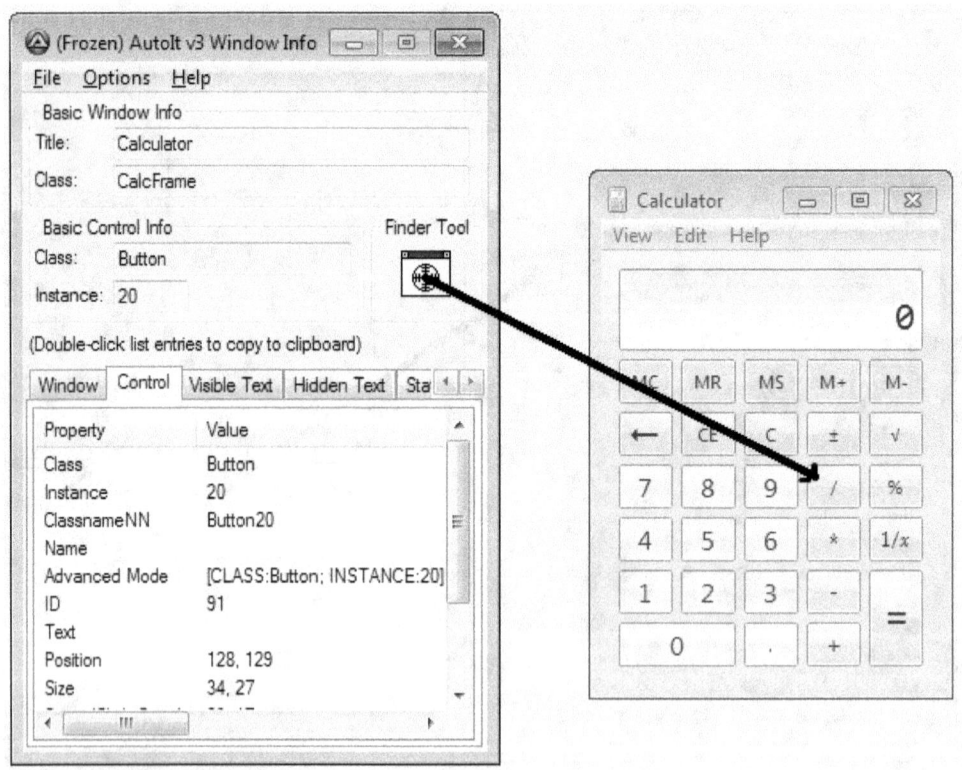

Fig 13.6Properties of button /

7) Properties of button 2

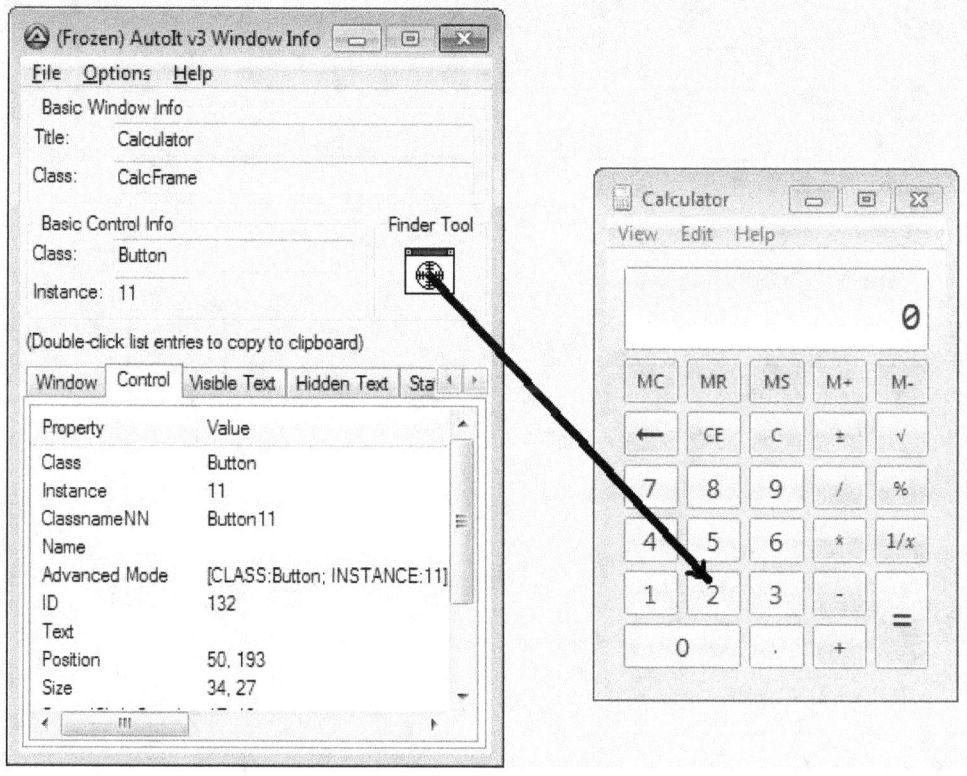

Fig 13.7Properties of button 2

It's time to automate the calculator with the help of the properties we determined so far.

```
1    ;Launch calculator
2    Run("calc.exe")
3    ;Wait for 2 seconds
4    Sleep(2000)
5    ;Click the button 8
6    ControlClick("Calculator","","[ID:138;INSTANCE:9; CLASS:Button]")
7    ;Wait of half second
8    Sleep(500)
9    ;Click the button 4
10   ControlClick("Calculator","","[ID:134;INSTANCE:4; CLASS:Button]")
11   Sleep(500)
12   ;Click the button *
13   ControlClick("Calculator","","[ID:92;INSTANCE:21; CLASS:Button]")
14   Sleep(500)
15

16   ;Click the button 4
17   ControlClick("Calculator","","[ID:134;INSTANCE:4; CLASS:Button]")
18   Sleep(500)
19   ;Click the button 0
20   ControlClick("Calculator","","[ID:130;INSTANCE:6; CLASS:Button]")
21   Sleep(500)
22   ;Click the button =
23   ControlClick("Calculator","","[ID:121;INSTANCE:28; CLASS:Button]")
24   Sleep(500)
25   ;Click the button /
26   ControlClick("Calculator","","[ID:91;INSTANCE:20; CLASS:Button]")
27   Sleep(500)
28   ;Click the button 2
29   ControlClick("Calculator","","[ID:132;INSTANCE:11; CLASS:Button]")
30   Sleep(500)
31   ;Click the button =
32   ControlClick("Calculator","","[ID:121;INSTANCE:28; CLASS:Button]")
33   Sleep(500)
```

Fig 13.8Calculator automation script

To compile the script, Select Tools -> Compile. A.exe file will be generated in the directory where the script exists.

On executing the .exe file, it will launch the calculator window and wait for 2 seconds. Then, the ControlClick function will start pressing buttons 8, 4, * ,4, 0, =,/,2.= with a half second delay so that it will be visible to the user during execution. Finally it displays the output.

Fig 13.9 Output

Conclusion

Thank you for reading this book. I hope this book helps beginners improve their programming knowledge. I feel honored to share this knowledge with my readers. I put great effort into narrating this book in a simple, easy and engaging way so that beginners can understand and grasp the content easily.

 I have a small request for you –please leave a review for my book and feel free to share your opinion, suggestions and corrections so that it will help me further improve the book.

Regards

Rajan

www.ingramcontent.com/pod-product-compliance
Lightning Source LLC
Chambersburg PA
CBHW072303200526
45168CB00014B/229